The Statutes of Henry VII. in Exact Facsimile, From the Very Rare Original, Printed by Caxton in 1489

Great Britain. Statutes

THE STATUTES

OF

HENRY VII.

IN EXACT FACSIMILE, FROM THE VERY RARE ORIGINAL, PRINTED BY CAXTON IN 1489.

EDITED, WITH NOTES AND INTRODUCTION,

BY

JOHN RAE,

MEMBER OF THE ROYAL INSTITUTION.

LONDON:
JOHN CAMDEN HOTTEN, 74 AND 75, PICCADILLY.
1869.

INTRODUCTION.

———∘⊶⊷∘———

THE following volume of Statutes, comprising those enacted in the first three Parliaments of Henry VII., is a facsimile of the earliest collection of English laws ever printed, and besides containing much information illustrative of the politics, trade, and domestic affairs of England, is further remarkable as being in our native tongue, and not in the Norman-French, which from the time of the Conquest had been employed for such purposes. It is a production of Caxton's press, and probably was one of the last works published by the father of our typography. The third Parliament of Henry VII. met in the year 1489, and Caxton died about 1491 or 1492, the record of his death appearing in the Account Book for that time of the churchwardens of St. Margaret's, Westminster. This book is in the Grenville collection, and within it is a slip of paper, on which appears the following autograph note of Mr. Grenville:

"Statutes of Henry 7, s. a. l. (Caxton).

"A small fragment of this volume was all that had been seen by Ames, or Herbert, or Dibdin till Lord Spencer was enabled to buy the only perfect copy, which was long considered as unique till this year of 1843, in which I purchased this beautiful and perfect copy : a detailed description of it is written by Dibdin for the *Gentleman's Magazine*, 1811, p. 232, being afterwards printed in Bib. Spencer, Vol. IV., p. 344."

Ames (see ed. 1810 by Herbert, with additions by Dibdin) says that Caxton published the Statutes made in the first, second, and third Parliaments of Henry VII., fo., type No. 3.

Lowndes gives amongst the works of Caxton, the Acts 1st, 2nd, and 4th of Henry VII.

Mr. Blades, in his Life and Typography of Caxton, states that only four perfect copies of the present work are known, viz. :

One in the Library of the Inner Temple, another known as Earl Spencer's, a third in the Grenville collection at the British Museum, and a fourth in the Imperial Library of Paris ; adding, however, that a copy is in the possession of A. B. Middleton, Esq., which, he observes, is imperfect, wanting all after signature e, j.

The first of these he describes as in tolerable preservation. In many places it is scribbled upon : is generally soiled ; the margins being in some places stained, and the latter leaves worm-eaten : all the typographical details agree with those of the Grenville copy.

With reference to the copy mentioned by Mr. Blades as being in the French Imperial Library, inquiries having been made of M. Vaschéreau, the Administrator General Director of that establishment, with a view to ascertain the condition of the work, that gentleman states there is no copy of Caxton's work in the Library, and never has been one, but that the Library contains a copy of Pynson's Nova Statuta (1497), a work which is noticed very disparagingly by the Editors of the Statutes of the Realm printed by order of Geo. III., in the year 1817. M. Vaschéreau also remarks that there is no copy of Caxton's work in the Bibliothèque Impériale du Louvre.

It is probable that Mr. Blades trusted to the report of some one less erudite than himself, and who confounded the productions of Caxton with those of another early English printer.

Thus the number of perfect copies is reduced to three ; the Spencer copy, it is to be remarked, differing in some respects from the other two : for example, the chapter in the latter headed, *Felde*, is in the former entitled *Felde in batteyll*: many of the chapters are in a different order of rotation. These discrepancies have been ascertained to exist, from Dibdin's printed statement of the contents, confirmed by the present Librarian at Althorpe. The Spencer copy has likewise some of the leaves stained by the mildew arising from damp, and is moreover slightly wormed. The Grenville copy, the original of our Facsimile, is in very beautiful preservation, and altogether far surpasses the other two copies. Mr. Blade remarks that there are thirty-one lines to a full page ; thirty-two lines, however, occasionally occur in all the copies. There is no place or date, printer's name, or any device impressed upon any of the copies.

Besides the above, it is probable that a few leaves may have been found in some collection, and which enabled Dibdin to give his account of the book, since no perfect copy was known to be then existent.

The period to which these Statutes refers is one of the most interesting in our national history. In the reign of Henry VII., the social state of England received an impetus, which ever since has been exercising a powerfully beneficial influence on the Institutions of the Country, and which has materially conduced to our present prosperity, and advanced civilization. During the greater part of the previous century the land was waste; Agriculture and Commerce were neglected; while savage rivalry, and discord, fermented by the long wars waged between the rival factions of York and Lancaster, had well nigh depopulated the country; but when the death of Richard III, and the marriage of Henry, the head of the house of Lancaster, with Elizabeth princess of York, had removed the jealousies, and consolidated the interests of the two families, and when, moreover, many of the turbulent Barons, who, during the time of strife and anarchy had revelled in lawless independence, were reduced by the force of necessity to submission, then the prospect of peace and general amelioration presented itself, which the King earnestly sought to realise. His endeavours were supported by the Commoners, who were clamorously desirous of asserting their rights, and securing their personal liberties against the unbearable inflictions of the Nobles. Henry was well fitted for the task thus undertaken. He was of a calm, deliberate and reserved disposition; full of energy and industry; loving order and peace without fearing war; his capacity was excellent, and, whatever were the motives which guided him in his policy, it is beyond dispute that most of his laws were good, and that he rendered the nation very eminent service. "Certainly," says Bacon, in his striking and masterly life of this prince, "his times for good commonwealth laws did excel, so as he may justly be celebrated for the best lawgiver to this nation after King Edward the First. For his laws (whoso marks them well) are deep and not vulgar : not made upon the spur of a particular occasion for the present, but out of providence for the future, to make the estate of his people still more and more happy, after the manner of the legislators in ancient and heroical times." This brilliant commendation, however, must be taken with some exception. Bacon himself, with his contemporaries generally, entertained very imperfect and erroneous ideas on some points of internal administration and the principles of commerce; it must also be remembered that the matured laws which now govern commercial transactions were wholly unknown in the fifteenth century. The laws framed by Henry VII, for the direction of the police, were conceived with better judgment than those he enacted for the regulation of commerce : this may be accounted for by the fact that the requirements of the internal administration of Justice lie on the surface, and a simple notion of order and equity will enable the legislator fully to grasp them; but the principles of commerce are more deeply seated and more complicated : long experience, deep reflection, and a sound discrimination alone can enable a statesman thoroughly to master their intricaces. Moreover, a longer interval is necessary to show the results of laws affecting trade and commerce, and these results often prove quite contrary to the anticipation. Thus it was with Henry's prohibitory laws, limitations, restrictions, and monopolies of trade, many of which were calculated seriously to retard the progress of commerce. It could not however be expected that one, who, in his early days, had been more conversant with war than with commerce, should be wholly in advance of his age on a subject requiring a combination of faculties seldom to be found in the capacities of Monarchs. Monopolies were characteristic of the time, and continued in vogue for more than two centuries after : grants of them formed one of the sources whence the crown drew money as a price of, or by means of which it rewarded or secured an adherent. Monopolies were never more freely created than in the reign of Elizabeth : the Lansdowne MSS. show that they were in daily request, when the great Lord Burleigh administered the affairs of the kingdom : Raleigh held a license to export broad and other cloths, and to vend wines. So far the fashion of the time, and, from the reign of Henry VII., it required more than three centuries of Time's teaching, ere the people could discover that the mutual adoption, by the family of nations, of the principles of freedom in trade, is the most powerful promoter of international prosperity.

Henry VII. assembled his first Parliament within three months after his coronation on Monday, November 7th, 1485 ; his reasons for calling this meeting were fourfold : 1st, To cause the crown to be entailed upon himself and his line (the Act passed for this purpose is not in the present volume; it is entitled Titulus Regis : but does not appear in any of the early printed collection of Statutes, but is inserted in the Petyt MS. in the Library of the Inner Temple) : 2nd, To have the numerous attainders of his adherents reversed, and to proclaim an amnesty for all acts of hostility committed by them for his benefit : 3rd, To attaint some of the principal leaders of the Yorkist party : 4th, Thereafter to calm and allay the fears of that party by an extensive pardon, well knowing in what danger a King stands from his subjects, when large numbers of them are conscious that their own safety is uncertain. Having thus secured the general peace of the country, Henry directed his attention to the security of his officers, and of all his subjects, particularly the Commoners. Numerous laws were framed for the repression of murder and manslaughter, crimes of frequent occurrence in consequence of the turbulence of the times; but his ever constant aim was to lessen the power and influence of the ancient nobility, and to create new families and churchmen; and as these recently ennobled were naturally more dependent upon him than were the old aristocracy who enjoyed large hereditary possessions, and wielded the influence of ancient names, he rightly judged that the prospect of further favours would render them still more active in his service and obsequious to his demands. In order to carry out his policy of depressing that ancient nobility whose interests so often antagonized with his own, and many of whom were possessed of privileges and jurisdictions dangerous to royal authority, the King caused laws to be enacted which tended materially to lessen their power. One of his first Statutes, for this object, was that against the giving of Livery (3 Henry VII., c. 1), and a Session scarcely passed during his reign without the operation of some enactment against engaging retainers, and giving them liveries and badges. This practice, which may appear of little importance to the interests of the State, had at that time grown to be a source of serious embarrassment to the crown. Many enactments relating to it were made even before the time of Henry VII. In the first year of the reign of Henry IV., ch. 17, the giving of liveries was forbidden except by the King, and even these were not to be worn but in his presence, except in times of war. This enactment was confirmed in the second year of his reign ; re-confirmed together with the 1st Statute of Rich. II. c. 7, in the seventh year, and all previous Statutes to the same effect were again ratified in the thirteenth year. By 8th Henry VI., c. 4, Justices of the Peace were directed to proceed against all persons transgressing the laws on this subject. A Livery generally consisted of a hat or hood, a badge, and a suit of clothes. In consequence of the feuds which this custom of giving Liveries engendered, the license to give them became an honour at last granted only to persons of uncommon distinction. The signs and tokens mentioned by the Statute were badges and cognizances ; badges were the master's device, crest or arms on a separate piece of cloth, (or, as in the time of Elizabeth, on silver), in the form of a shield, worn on the left sleeve, by domestics and retainers, and even by younger brothers, who wore the badge of the elder; this was generally continued till the time of James I., after which it was only worn by watermen, and servants of persons of distinction. The Royal watermen, when on duty, still wear it. Cognizances were sometimes knots or devices worn in the cap or on the chest ; some of the Royal servants wore the King's arms both on the breast and on the back. Reteyndres appear to have been the agreements, verbal, or written, by which the retainers, sometimes called Retinue, (Retynew, vide the Statute entitled *Reteyndour*) were engaged or retained. The possession of Retainers and Liveries led to much abuse ; great Lords were in the habit of engaging a number of retainers, who were not maintained as servants, but were trained to warlike exercises. Thus we read that, in the reign of Henry VI., the Earl of Warwick frequently came to London attended by six hundred men attired in red jackets, embroidered both on the breast, and on the back with two ragged staves in saltire —the Earl's badge. In his house six oxen were often eaten at breakfast, and every tavern in the neighbourhood kept open doors: for whoever had any acquaintance in the house of the Earl, might there have as much roast or boiled meat as he could prick and carry on a long dagger.

In the reign of Queen Mary some of the great Lords had two hundred retainers, but Elizabeth would not permit any person to secure more than one hundred. Thus numbers of men were maintained in vicious idleness, which naturally generated a restless martial spirit, so that they were always ready to assist their masters in every undertaking, whether lawful or otherwise. The nobility had long vied with each other in increasing the number of their retainers, and it required all the energy and rigour of the King to extirpate the evil. An amusing anecdote is told of his vigilance in this respect. The Earl of Oxford, the King's favourite general, in whom he always placed great and deserved confidence, having splendidly entertained him at the castle of Heningham, was desirous of making a parade of his magnificence at the departure of the royal guest, and ordered all his retainers, in their liveries, to be drawn up in two lines, that their appearance might be more splendid and imposing. " My lord," said the King, " I have heard much of your hospitality, but the truth far exceeds the report. These handsome gentlemen and yeomen, whom I see on both sides of me, are no doubt your menial servants?" The Earl smiled, but professed that his fortune was too narrow for such magnificence. "They are most of them," rejoined he, "my retainers, who are come to do me service at this time, when they know I am honoured with the presence of your Highness." The King started a little, and replied, "By my faith, my lord, I thank you for your good cheer, but I must not allow my laws to be broken in my sight. My attorney must speak with you." In consequence of this conversation with the attorney, Oxford is said to have paid no less than fifteen thousand marks as a composition for his offence.

It is related by Lloyd, in his *Statesmen and Favorites of England*, that Wolsey kept 500 servants, among whom were 9 or 10 Lords, 15 Knights, and 40 Esquires. Henry Lord Marquis Dorset, father of Lady Jane Grey, says in his depositions, taken by the Protector Somerset against the Lord Admiral, anno 1548, "the admiral devising with me to make me strong in my country, advised me to keep a good house, and asked me what friends I had in my country; to whom I made answer that I had divers servants that were gentlemen, etc." From a passage in Smith's *Berkeley Papers*, it appears that even ladies gave liveries; in an account of the journey of Isobel Marchioness of Berkeley, 8th Henry VIII., to London, there occurs, " Item first, xxx. of her livery ;" virtually the husbands of such of these women as were married, must have been retainers of her Ladyship's house ; probably such were also the male relatives of the single women.* In the Defence of Coney-catching, 1592, the following passage occurs, " Sirha, although

* To establish the fact of the general prevalence of this custom, it may be remarked that on the marriage of Charles Duke of Burgundy, with the Lady Margaret of York, when the bride arrived at the Duke's court at Bruges, our author, Caxton, was one of her retinue. He continued in her service for some time afterwards, and received a yearly fee, together with other advantages.

you have a Livery on your backe, and a cognizaunce to countenaunce you withal, and beare the port of a gentleman, yet I see you are a false knave, etc."

The preamble to the statute concerning the Giving of Liveries furnishes a remarkable picture of the state of the nation at that time : " The kyng our sayd souereyn lord remēbreth how bi vnlawfull mayntenaunces gyuynges of liueres signes & tokens & reteyndres by endêtures promyses othes wrytinges or otherwyse embrasaries of his subgettes vntrue demeanynges of shireffes in makynge of panelles & other vntrue retournes by takynge of money. by iurries. by grete riottes & vnlawfull assemblees. The police & good rule of this reame is almost subdued, and for the nonū punyshynge of thise incōuenyences, and by occasion of the premysses noo thyng, or lityll maye be fonde by enquerry. Wherby the lawes of the lond in execucion maye take lityll effecte to thencres of murdres robberies periuries & vnsuertees of all men leuynge and losses of their londes and goodes, to the grete dyspleysur of Almyghty God." Such a condition of affairs doubtless required great discretionary power in the sovereign, and this Henry VII. fully possessed, for scarcely ever had any king of England been invested with a sway more absolute. In order to eradicate the evils enumerated in the above preamble, the authority of the Star-chamber was established, or rather its powers were enlarged and confirmed by Act of Parliament. Bacon describes this Court as " one of the sagest and noblest institutions of this kingdom." Without by any means fully endorsing this opinion, it must be admitted that it was a kind of jurisdiction which partly suited the rude state of the nation, and, in the words of Hume: "The establishment of the Star-chamber, or the enlargement of its power in the reign of Henry VII.,

might have been as wise as the abolition of it in that of
Charles I."

But the most remarkable law of this whole reign
is the Statute entitled " De Finibus," by which the
nobility and gentry acquired the power of breaking
the ancient entails, and of alienating their estates. This
law, joined to the elegance, and luxury which was
gradually introduced, served to ruin the great for-
tunes of the barons, but at the same time increased the
wealth and importance of the commons. A previous
statute prepared the way for the law, which was enacted
against enclosures and " for keeping up the houses of
husbandry " (4 Hen. VII. c. 19). Enclosures at that
time began to be more numerous, in consequence of
which arable land was turned into pastures, which
were easily managed by a few herdsmen. Tenancies for
years, lives, and at will, such as were held mostly by the
yeomanry, were turned into demesnes. This had the
effect of diminishing the towns, churches, tithes, &c.
What the King felt most acutely was the diminution and
decay of the subsidy and taxes; for, as Bacon says : " The
more gentlemen, ever the lower books of subsidies." It
was not, however, advisable to forbid enclosures, for that
would have been obstructing the improvement of the pa-
trimony of the kingdom, nor could tillage be compulsory,
as that depended on the nature of the soil. Therefore the
King took a course by which he obtained his object in an
indirect manner. An ordinance was framed, whereby all
farms to which twenty acres of land and upwards were
attached, should be maintained for ever, together with a
sufficient portion of land to be used with them, and
to be held un-severed. This, upon forfeiture, was
to be taken by seizure of the land itself by the King

and lords of the fee, with half the profits, till the houses and lands were restored. By this means, as the houses were maintained they required tenants, and the land being attached, it became necessary for that tenant to be a man of some substance, who would keep the plough going and support hinds and servants. Hence arose our vigorous yeomanry, a class between the gentry and the cottagers or peasants : "men bred not in a servile and indigent manner, but free and plentyfull."

The statute against "Giving of Livery", also ordained the King's suit for murder to be carried on within a year and a day, whilst before this time it did not usually commence till after that period had elapsed, during which interval the friends of the murdered person frequently compounded with the murderer, who by this means escaped justice. Numerous other excellent statutes, for the administration of justice and the government of the kingdom, were made during the three parliaments of which the present work treats. It was made felony to abduct women ; the admission to bail was more strictly regulated ; fraudulent transfers were declared null and void ; and many other wise laws were enacted. One statute is somewhat curious : by an Act it was declared felony in any servant of the King to conspire against the life of the Steward, Treasurer, or Comptroller of the King's household, even though the design was not followed by any overt act. This law, it was thought, had been procured by the Lord Chancellor, Archbishop Morton, who, being of a stern and haughty disposition, and knowing that he had many mortal enemies at Court, provided it for his own safety. The real purport of his Act he tried to disguise by making it general, and communicating the privilege to all other counsellors and peers; yet he did not dare to extend it further than to the King's household, lest the gentlemen and commons should have taken umbrage, and considered their ancient liberty and the clemency of the law invaded if the will in any case of felony should be accounted equal to the deed. Yet the reason which the Act gives, "the destruction of the King and the undoing of the realm," is alike to subjects as to servants in Court. "However," says Bacon, " it seems this sufficed the Lord Chancellor's turn at this time, but yet he lived to need a general law, for that he grew afterwards so odious to the country as he was then to the Court."

As before observed, many of King Henry's statutes relating to commerce and manufacture, and intended to promote their welfare, were merely clogs and obstructions. The great error of the period, and which it occupied ages to eradicate, was the restraint upon industry, in consequence of the jealousy of the corporations and mysteries. Some of these limitations the King enlarged, but not sufficiently so as to admit, that competition and emulation alone can ensure continuous progress. Another great error common to the times was that of fixing the prices of various commodities. Thus, with a view to promote archery, it was enacted that no long bows should be sold at a higher price than 6s. 4d. Prices were also affixed to the charges for cloth : a yard of the best scarlet cloth was not to be dearer than 16s., and a yard of cloth of any other colour not more than 11s. "A *rare* thing to set prices by statute, especially on our home commodities," says Bacon, who admired the wisdom of this Act. But the effect of such laws is often different from that expected by their authors : for as it is impossible to fix a standard of excellence in articles of this kind, so will the effect necessarily be that the articles supplied at the minimum statute price must be of a minimum quality. Again, the idea of restricting the price of produce is futile, for the amount of available material cannot be fixed ; and if its supply be scanty, one of two things must result, either the price of the product will be enhanced, or the manufacture must be abandoned. The preamble to another Act ("Price of Hats and Bonnets," 4 Hen. VII. c. 9) shows the fallacy of this system of trade protection, or rather limitation ; for, being united by the bonds of a craft, mystery, or corporation, the maker could govern the market, and demand his own unreasonable prices. In this manner the hatters and cappers are stated to have been in the habit of selling hats and caps, which cost them no more than sixteen-pence, at prices varying from three to five shillings ; this profit, the King thought, was exorbitant, and he therefore reduced the best hats to the price of 1s. 8d., and the best caps to 2s. 8d. each. Equally useless and vexatious were the laws enacted during this reign, prohibitory of the exportation of money, plate, bullion, and even jewelry. Not only foreign traders, but also merchants from Ireland and the Channel Islands, were compelled to expend the proceeds of their sales in England, upon the native commodities of the realm, which was much like reducing commerce to barter. Such precautions, necessarily, were ineffectual, and only caused more of the prohibited articles to be exported. Severe regulations were also made against taking interest on money, which was designated by the name of Usury, Dry Exchange, and New Chevisance, and is described in the statute as a "damnable bargain," the unavoidable consequence of which would be "the common hurt of this land and the great displeasure of God." By the same sweeping Act, all contracts by which interest was paid for the loan of money were branded as usurious, and even the profits of exchange were prohibited on the grounds of religion and political economy. These illogical views continued to be maintained for more than a century and a half after this period. Even so late as the reign of Charles the First, Justice Rastall described interest or usury as " a gain of anything above the principal or that which was lent, exacted only in consideration of the loane, whether it be corn, meat, apparel, wares, or such like, as money." He then proceeded to impress upon " those who think themselves religious and good Christians " that they cannot with a good conscience take even ten per cent., which the statute then allowed, inasmuch as the Scripture says: " Lend, looking for nothing thereby, whereby it is forbidden to take one penny above the principall." The condemnation of interest for the use of money may be ascribed to the ecclesiastics, who were Judges and Advocates in the Civil Courts, giving rise to the adage *Nullus Clericus nisi Causidicus*, and who imported into their arguments and decisions matter from the Ecclesiastical law unknown alike to the Statute and the Common-law of England. The nobility and the other landowners were willing to acquiesce in the doctrine, believing, as they did, in the supremacy of land, and the Sovereign was equally ready to submit to the popular prejudice, engendered and fostered as it was by the feudal system; yet it is somewhat surprising that a Prince so astute as Henry VII. should not have penetrated this mist of error, since he is said to have accumulated and left no less than £1,800,000, most of it under his own key and keeping at Richmond, where he died. Blackstone remarks that the distinguishing characteristic of this reign was that of amassing treasure in the king's coffers. See Baker's *Chronicles.* Locke in his *Treatise on Interest* says " my money is apt in trade by the industry of the borrower to produce more than 6 per cent., (then the legal rate), to the borrower, as well as your land, by the labour of your tenant, is apt to produce more fruits than the rent comes to, and therefore deserves to be paid for, as well as land, by a yearly rent."

Henry VIII., in the 37th year of his reign, limited the interest on loans to ten per cent. per annum; Edward VI. abrogated this law, and it was enacted that no interests upon land could be received, and if any were taken the principal was forfeited to the crown, with fine and ransom at the king's pleasure; in the 13th Elizabeth this last act was repealed and that of Henry VIII. revived. By a statute of Queen Elizabeth (13 Eliz. c. 8) it was enacted that he who took even under ten per cent. forfeited the interest so taken. It was only by 21 Jam. c. 17, that interest amounting to ten per cent. was allowed; "upon like cause," observes an old writer, "that moved Moses to give a bill of divorce to the Israelites, as namely, to avoid a greater mischief and for the hardnesse of their hearts."

The foregoing remarks apply to a few of the more important statutes contained in this collection, some of which have exercised a powerful influence in directing this country to that course of commerce, police, and cultivation in which it has ever since persevered. It was from such infantine attempts that the nation, by constant progression, has happily established " the most perfect and most accurate system of liberty that ever was found compatible with government." Not of less interest are some of the laws made by this Sovereign for the police of the kingdom, and from the preambles to them we become conversant with the condition of the country and the state of the people at the period of their enactment. The statute " Against Hunters," for instance, speaks of strange practices, and describes the " inordinate and unlawful hunting," particularly in Kent and Sussex, by divers persons, who went in great numbers into parks and forests, and there hunted by night and by day, " some with painted faces, some with masks, and otherwise disguised and in manner of war arrayed," shewing at the same time that game-laws were then as unpopular with the Commonalty as they had been in previous, and were in subsequent times. Again, the statute for " Commissions of Sewers " gives a remarkable picture of England, where, in that day, in the counties of Gloucester, Somerset, and elsewhere, " by the increase of waters, divers lands and tenements in great quantity " were flooded and destroyed by inundations. So menacing was this evil that it threatened speedily to accomplish " the decrease and destruction of the livelyhood of the King, of the Church, and of other true liege people of this realm." Many things contributed to this condition of affairs, for during the protracted wars, water-courses had been neglected and become choked, dykes were broken down, and other accidents of the same nature had happened, the natural consequences of depopulation. Such things at least, we see, occurred on the banks of the Thames, where, according to the Statute "for the Mayor

of London," within a few years, by tempests and inundations, numerous issues, breaches, and creeks had become
formed, and overrun pastures, meadows, and the
grounds of divers persons. We obtain a further insight
into the misery caused by civil war, and a vicious social
system, in the remarkable preamble to the statute concerning the Isle of Wight, which, in its sober, formal
official phraseology, gives a most striking picture of the
utter desolation of a portion of the land now remarkable
for its genial climate and generally luxurious aspect.
This, in a great measure was attributable to the increasing
practice of enclosing lands and forming large demesnes.
Against this evil, laws are ineffectual. Unless actuated
by exceptional motives, proprietors will not encourage
excessive populousness. Until the time of the Commonwealth there were numerous laws and edicts against depopulation, as also many Acts against the overcrowding of
London, but it does not appear that these enactments
were ever rigorously enforced. The natural course of
improvement at last provided the remedy.

It may be added that Henry fostered other arts of
peace: he greatly enlarged the Royal house at Green-
wich, built by Humphrey Duke of Gloucester, giving
it the name of Placentia; he also rebuilt Baynard's
Castle, and the Palace at Sheen, now called Richmond,
where he died; he finished the Savoy, and gave it lands
for the support of 200 poor people; he erected no less
than six houses for Franciscan Friars; he also gave to
posterity his beautiful chapel at Westminster, which
building Leland calls the Miracle of the World. The
example of the Monarch was largely followed by his
nobles.

A consideration of these old and well-nigh forgotten

laws is interesting, not only to the historical and anti-
quarian student, but also to the general reader.

We enter the Chamber of the Past, and from the
shelves take down the record of the times long since
gone. A quaint volume, hoary with the dust of ages, is
carefully and reverently freed from its thick coating,
and its pages opened. Although at first the character of
the typography and diction appears strange and uncouth,
a little patient pondering reveals to us matter and thought,
rich with the lore of antiquity; the dead seem to live
again, and the past comes laden with lessons to the
present. From the little volume, time-worn and unpre-
tending, start out vivid pictures of the old days; the
troubles that perplexed; the abuses that clung around
the customs of our forefathers; the incidents that
marked their every day life come faithfully before us.
We identify ourselves with them, not altogether without
a suspicion that much of the abuse then existent is closely
analagous to the evil of our own day. Even if we are
filled with the complacence arising from the present
superiority of knowledge and advanced civilization, we
may, nevertheless, with much advantage mark the labours of our ancestors, in their efforts to construct laws
adapted to the exigencies of the times.

Valuable instruction may be gathered from these old
statutes, even though we, in the plenitude of our en-
lightenment, may be disposed to question their judgment
and deny their efficacy. Grotesque blundering in legis-
lation is not altogether confined to the times of Caxton, and before we depreciate these ancient laws, we
must surrender, and consign many of the darlings of
modern law to the region of the impracticable and the
absurd.

We do well, then, to read and cherish these old enactments, recognising them as the honest endeavour of the men of the time to combat, and if possible alleviate the abuses then afflicting our brave old land.

"An acquaintance, with the ancient periods of our government," says Hume, " is chiefly *useful* by instructing us to cherish our present constitution, from a comparison or contrast with the condition of those distant times. And it is also *curious*, by shewing us the remote and commonly faint originals of the most finished and most noble institutions, and by instructing us in the great mixture of accident which commonly concurs with a small ingredient of wisdom and foresight in erecting the complicated fabric of the most perfect government."

JOHN RAE.

Chislehurst, Kent,
    June, 1869.

¶ The kynge our souereyn lorde henry the seuenth after the conquest by the grace of god kyng of Englonde & of Fraunce and lorde of Irlonde at his parlyamet holden at Westmynster the seuenth daye of Nouembre in the first yere of his reigne/ To thonour of god & holy chirche/and for the comen profyte of the royame/bi thassent of the lordes spirituell & temporell/and the comens in the sayd parliamet assembled/and by auctorite of the sayd parlpamente/hath co to be made certein statutes & ordenaunces in maner & fourme folowyng/

¶ Fermedowne

First that where dyuerse of the kynges subgettes hauyng cause of accyon by Fermedowne in the descendre or elles in the remaynodre by force of ony taill of and for londes & tenementes ben defrauded & delaied of the said accions. And ofte tymes wythout remedy by cause of feoffemetis made of the same londes and tenementes to persones vnknowen to thentent that the demaudantes sholde not knowe apenst whom they shall take their accion/ It is ordeyned stablysshed & enacted/by the aduyce of the lordes spyrituell & temporell and the comens in the sayd parlya ment assembled and by auctorite of the same that the demaundant in euery suche caas haue his accion apenst the pernour or pernours of the profytes of the londes or tenementes demaunded wherof ony persone or persones ben enfeoffed to his or their vse/And the same pernour or pernours named as tenaunt or tenautes in the said accion haue the same vourchers/And their lien there vpon eide p per/and all other auantages as the same pernour or pernours shold haue had if they were tenautes in dede or as their feoffes shold de haue had if the same accion had be conceyued ayest theim

And yf it fortune ony persone to dyscese soo hauyng feof﹐
fes to thuse of hym. or of his heires/ the sayd heyre beynge
wythin age/Apenst whom suche accion is brought as per﹐
nour.therinne the same heire haue his age in the sayd accy﹐
on conueyd apenste hym/ And all other auautages as yf
his aunceftre had wyed ceased of the sayd londes & tenemen
tes soo in demaude/And also it is ordeyned bi the sayd auc
torite/ that all recouerees as shall be in ony suche accyons
agayne suche pernour or pernours.and their heires and their
sayd feoffes and their heires & the cofeoffes of the sayd per﹐
nours & their heires as though the said pernour or pernours
were tenautes in dede. or feoffes to their Vse. or their heires
as is aboue sayd of the free holde of the sayd londes & tene﹐
mentis/at ony tyme of the sayd accyon Vsed/

℩ Apenste strangers made deynzens to paye custo﹐
mes/ &c

℩ Item where in tyme past dyuerse grautes haue be ma
de by kynge Edwarde aswell by his lettres patentes as bi
actes of parliament to dyuerse marchautis strangers borne
oute of this reame to be deynszeyns/Wherby they haue & re﹐
ioyce suche fredomes & libertees as woth deynszeyns borne
wythin this reame.aswell in abatement of their custome
Whiche they shold bere yf they were noo deynszeyns as in bi
ynge & sellyng of their marchaundyses. to their grete auay﹐
le & lucre/And ofte tymes suffre other strangers not deyn﹐
szeyns deceptfully to shippe and carie grete and notable sub
staunce of marchaundyse. in their names/By the Whiche the
sayd goodes be freed of custome in lyke Wyse/as they were
goodes of a deynszen. where of righte they oughte to paye
custome as the goodes of straungers .by the Whyche they

be gretly auaunſed in rickeſſe and hauour. And after they
be ſoo enricheð for the mooſt parte / they conueye their ſelfe
wyth their ſayð goodes in to their owne countrees. Wherin
they ben naturelly borne / to the grete enpouerſhyng of this
reame / and to the grete hurte and defraude of the kynges
highnes in payment of his cuſtomes. Wherefore it is en=
acteð ſtabliſheð and orðeyned by the aðuyſe of the ſayð lor=
des ſpprituell and temporell and comens in the ſayð parlia
mente aſſembleð and by auctorite of the ſame / that ony per
ſone maðe or here after to be maðe ðenyzen pay for his mar
chandiſe like cuſtome & ſubſiðye as he ought or ſholðe paye
afore that he were maðe ðenyzen / ony lettres patentes or o=
ther orðenaüce by parliamēt or other wyſe, contrary to thys
maðe, not wythſtondynge.

¶ (Noo protectyon be alowed in ony court at Calays)

¶ Item the kynge our ſouereyne lorðe / by thaðuyſe of the
lorðes ſpprituell and temporell / and at the prayer of the co
mens in the ſaið parliament aſſembleð, and by auctorite of
the ſame hath enacteð orðeyneð and ſtabliſheð / that noo pro
tectyon be here after alowable ne aloweð in the courte byfo
re the Mayre, conſtables and feliſhyp of marchauntes / of
the ſtaple at calays / ne in the courte byfore the lientenaunte
conſtable and feliſhip of marchauntes of the ſame ſtaple
ne in the courte byfore the mayre and his bretherne of the
ſame towne of calays, nor in ony other courte or courtes
wythin the ſame towne, or marckes there in ony actyon
ſueð / or here after to be ſueð by ony of the ſayð marcha
untes, their factours / ſeruauntes or attorney s / ayenſte ony
of the ſayð marchauntes / their factours ſeruauntes / or
attorneys.

a   iiij

¶ Correccyns of prestes for Incontynence.

¶ Item for the more sure and lyke reformacyon of pres
tes clerkes and religyous men culpable or by theyr demery
tes openly noysed of incontynente lyuynge in theyr bodyes
contrary to theyr ordre/ It is enacted ordeyned and establi
shed by the aduyse and assente of the lordes spiryduell and
temporell and comens in the sayd parliamente assembled.
and by auctorite of the same. that it be lawfull to all arche;
byshops & byshops and other ordynaries hauynge epysco
pall iurisdiccion to punysse and chastice suche preestes cler
kes and religyous men beynge wythin the boundes of the
ir Iurisdiccion as shall be commytte afore theym by examy
nacion/ and other lawfull prooff/ requysite by the lawe of
the chircke of aduoutre fornycacyon incest/ or ony other fles
sly incontynency/By commyttynge theym to warde and pry
son there to abyde/for suche tyme as shall be thoughte to the
yr descressions conuenyent for the qualyte and quantite of
their trespasses. And that none of the sayd archebysshops
bysshops or other ordynaries a forsayd be therof chargeable
of to or vpon ony accyon of false or wrongfull imprysone
ment/ but that they be vtterly therof dyscharged in ony of
the cases aforsayd.by vertue of this acte/

¶ Ayenste Tanners and Cordyners
¶ Item that where Tanners in dyuerse partyes of this
reame vsen wythin theym selfe the mystere of curryng and
blackynge of lether insuffyciently/And also lether insuffy
ciently tanned/ and the same lether soo insuffyciently wro
ughte/as well in tannynge as in corryynge/ and blackyng

they put to sale in dyuerse fayres and markettes and other
places to grete decepte and hurte of the kynges liege people
And also where it was ordeyned and stablisshed at the par
liament holden at Westmynster the seconde yere of the reyg;
ne of kynge Henry the seuenth amonge other/that noo cor
delwener nor none other to his vse sholde ocuppe the myste;
rie of a tanner whilst he occuppied the mysterie of a cordwe;
ner vnder peyne of forfeyture of euery hyde soo tanned by
hym.or by ony other to his vse.vi. shelinges and viij. pens
And that euery tanner sholde also forfeyte for euery hide
by hym tanned Insuffycyendy vi. shelinges viij pens/as in
the same statute more pleynly appereth/   The kynge
our sayd souereyne lorde of his noble grace. by the aduyce &
assente of the lordes spyrituell & temprell. and at the pray;
er of his comens in this presente parliamente assembled
and by auctoritye of the same parliamente/ in eschuyng of
all suche decepces hath ordeyned and stablisshed that the sayd
ordenaunce made in the sayd seconde yere of kynge Henry
the seuenth. be and stonde in his full force & strength and
be put in due execucyon in all poyntes   And ouer that
by the sayd aduyce and auctorite/hath ordeyned and stabli;
shed that noo tanner whiles he occuppeth the mystere of a
tanner.nor none other to his vse from the feste of the ascen
sion of our lorde nexte comynge. vse the mystere of coriour/
nor blacke roo lether to be putte to sale/ vnder the peyne of
forfeyture for euery hide by the sayd tanner soo coried vi. she;
linges viij pens / And that noo corier of lether take vpon
hym/to corie ony hyde of lether/But suche as is a fore suffy;
ciendy tanned/vpon peyne to lese for euery hyde soo coryed
iij. shelinges iiij. pens/the one parte of the sayd forfeyture &
a   iiij

officers or mynisters of the sayd late duke/none accion be
mayntened. ne mayntenable apenst theym or ony of theym.
wythoute the kynges specyall licence. in that byhalfe optey
ned/ Prouyded allwaye that this presente acte extende not
ne in ony wyse be auaytlable to ony persone or persones aboue
specifyed of in or for ony murdre or rape of ony other
than was done the daye of the sayd felde or of ony dyssm
commytted or done by theym or ony of theym in ony wyse.
Prouyded also that this acte extende not. nor be preiudyci
all to ony persone or persones whiche had the saufgarde of
the kynge our souereyne lorde/ generall or speciall for ony
robberies trespasses/ or ony other Iniuries won or commytted
to theym or ony of theym after the saufgarde made/ Vnder
his pryue seale or sygnet or other warraunt suffycient pro
uyded allway þ this acte ne none other in this present parli
amente made or to be made be not hurtefull ne preiudyciatte
Vnto Elizabeth Wyndesore wedowe. late wyfe of Thomas
Wyndesore esquyer Edwarde Cheseman and sir Iohn Co
ket prest execuiours of the testament of the sayd Thomas
Wyndesore/ of or for ony robberie respasse or other offence
won Vnto the sayd Thomas in his liffe/But that the sayd
Elizabeth Edwarde and Iohn Coket maye haue and pur
sue actyon or actions apenst all maner persone or persones
ioyntly and seueratty for the sayd robberyes trespasses and
offences/And eche of theym by whatsomeuer name or na
mes the sayd Thomas Wyndesore the sayd Elizabeth Ed
warde Cheseman and Iohn Coket was or be named.
This acte or ony other acte in this present parliament ma
de or to be made (Notwythstandynge .

⸿ Item for as mocke as afore this tyme dyuerse ordena
unces and statutes haue be made in dyuerse parliamentes
holden in this reame for the punycyon of inordynate and
vnlawfull huntynges/in forest parkes/ and in warrēnes
wythin the sayd reame. Whiche statutes ⁊ ordynaunces not
wythstondynge dyuerse persones in grete nombre. some with
peynted faces/some wyth vysours/ and otherwyse dysgysed
to thentent they sholde not be knowen ryotously and in ma
ner of werre arrayed haue often tymes in late dayes hun
ted as well by nyghte as by daye in dyuerse forestes par:
kies and warrennes in dyuerse places of this reame/And
in especyall in the countye of kente surrey and suffer. By co
lour wherof haue ensued in tymes past grete and haynous
rebellyons insurreccyons Ryottes robberies murders and
other inconuenyences. to the preuocacyon and ensample of
ryottous and euyll dysposed persones of this reame/in su:
che wyse to offende. Whiche offenses colde not be duely pu:
nysshed afore this tyme accordynge to the sayd statutes orde
naunces ⁊ lawes of this sayd reame. by cause the sayd mis
doers by reason of their sayd paynted faces/ vysours and o:
ther dysgysynges colde not be knowen   The kynge
our sayd souereyne lorde of his noble and habundance grace
in consideracyon of the premysses/ by the aduyse and assent
of the lordes spyrituell and temporell at the supplycacyon
of the comens in the sayd parliamēt assembled and by auc
toryte of the same/that at euery suche tyme as informacyon
shall be made of ony suche vnlawfull huntynges by nyght
or wyth paynted faces bere after to be done . to ony of the

peas/ of the countee where ony suche huntynges shalle be
had of ony persone to be suspect therof/That than it be law
full to ony of the same counsell oz Justyces of peas/ to
whome suche enformacyon shall be made/ to make a warra
unte to the Shyrrof of suche countye. or to ony constable. bay
le/ oz other offycez wythin the same Countye. to take and ar
reste the same persone or persones/of whom suche enforma;
cion shall be made. And to haue hym or theym afore the
maker of the sayd warraunte/ oz ony other of the kynges
sayd counsell oz Justyces of his peas of the same countye
And that the sayd counseyllour, or Justyce of peas/ afore
whom suche persone oz persones shall be broughte/by his dis
crecyon haue power to exampn hym or theym/soo brought
afore the sayd counseyllour or iustyces.of the sayd huntyng
and of the sayd woers in that behalfe. And yf the same per
sone wylfully cocele the sayd hutinges/oz ony persone with
hym defectyue therin/that thenne the same concealement be a
penst eueri suche persone soo concelyng. felonye. And the sa
me felony to be enquyred of. and determyned as other felo;
nyes wythin this reame haue vsed to be/And yf be thenne
confesse the trouth/and all that he shall be exampned of and
knoweth in that behalfe / that thenne the same offences of
huntynges by hym done be as ayenst the kynge our souer
yn lorde But trespasse fynably by reason of the same confessi
on at the nexte generall sessions of the peas. to be holden in
the same coutye by the kyngis iustyce of the same sessyons
there to be sessed/ And yf ony rescusse or disobeysaunce be
made to ony persone. hauynge auctoryte to do execu;
cyon or iustyce by ony suche warrante by ony persone

the whiche ſoo ſholde be arreſted/ Soo that execucion of the
ſame warrant therby be not had that thenne the ſame reſcu
ſe and diſobeyſaunce be felony enqurable/ and determyna=
ble as is aſore ſayd/ And ouer this it is enacted and ſta
blyſſhed by the ſayd auctorite. that yf ony perſone or perſo=
nes bere after be commytted of ony ſuche huntynges wyth
peynted faces byſoures or otherwyſe dyſguyſed to thentent
they ſholde not be knowen. or of vnlawfull huntynge in ti
me of nyghte. that thenne the ſame perſone or perſones ſoo
commytted haue like punycion as he or they ſholde haue/ yf he
or they were competed of felony/

℞ For reperacyons of the Nauee.

℞ Item in the ſayd parliament/ it was called to remem=
braunce of the grete mynyſſhynge and decaye/ that hath be
now of late tyme of the nauye wythin this reame of Eng
londe. and Idleneſſe of the maryners wythin the ſame. By the
whiche this noble reame. within ſhort pwceſſe of tyme wyth
oute reformacion be had therin. ſhall not be of habylite and
power to deffende it ſelfe. Wherefore at the prayer of the ſa
yd compns/ the kynge our ſouerayne lorde by the aduyſe
of the lordes ſpprituell and temperell in this ſayd preſent
parliamente aſſembled. and by auctorite of the ſame/ It is
enacted ordeyned and eſtabliſſhed/ that noo maner of perſone
of what degree or condycion that he be of. bye nor ſelle wyth
in this ſayd reame/ Irlonde. wales calays/ or the marches
therof. or Berwyk. from the feſt of Myghelmas next now
compng. ony maner wynes of the growynge of the duchie
of Guyen or of Gaſcoygne/ but ſuche wynes as ſhalle
be auentured and broughte in an Engliſſhe / Iryſſhe or
Walſſhe mannys hyppe or ſhyppes/   And
that the maryners of the ſame engliſſhe Iriſſhe or walſſhe

men fyve the more parte /Or men of calays or of the mar=
ches of the same . and that vpon peyne of forfeiture. of the
same wynes soo boughte or solde contrary to this acte the
oon halfe of that forfeiture to be to the kynge our souereyn
lorde. and that other halfe to the fynder of that forfeiture/
This acte & ordenauce to endure bytwix this & the begyn=
nynge of the next parliamēt. Sauyng allwaye to the kyng
his prerogatyue.

¶ Sylke Werke

¶ Item that where in the parliamēt late holden at westmyn
ster the xx. day of Januarij the xij pere of kyng Edwarde
the fourth/It was enacted ordeyned & stablysshed by auctory
te of the sayd late parliamēt vpon many & grete consideracy
ons and lamētable compleyntes contepned in the same acte
that noo marchaūt stranger nor other after the fest of Es=
ter than next compng sholde brynge in to this reame of En
gelonde to be solde ony corses gyroles rybandes laces calle
sylke or colepn silke/throwen or wroughte vpon peyn of for
feiture therof / or of the value therof/ in whos handes they
shall be foūde/the oon halfe of the sayd forfeiture. to be vnto
the kyng our souereyn lorde and that other halfe/to be vnto
hym or theym of his subgettis the whiche shall sease the sa
me. or sue for the same by accyon of det by writte at comen
lawe/by bylle or pleynt after the custume of the cyte or tow
ne where it shall happen hereafter ony suche forfeyture to
falle or be. And that the deffendaūt in ony suche accyon be
not amytted by wage or do his lawe.Nor that ony protec=
cion nor essoyne in the seruyce of the kynge for ony suche de
fendaunt be alowed . The sayd acte to endure for iij. peres
than nexte ensuynge the sayd feste . The whiche acte after=
warde in the parliamēt holden by Richarde the thirde late in

dee and not in right kynge of Englonde was graunted ꝫ
ordeyned to be ꝫ stonde good auaillable ꝫ effectuell vnto the
ende of the sayd iiij yeres and from thende of the same iiij.
yeres vnto thende ꝫ terme of v. yeres than nexte ensuynge
The whiche sayd iiij yeres conteyned in the said first acte/
shal fynysshe ꝫ expire/at the fest of esterne/the whiche shall
be in the yere of our lorde god. M. CCCC. lxxxvij. The
kynge our sayd souereyn lorde that now is by auctorite of
this his aforesaid parlemēt hath ordeyned that the sayd ac
te ꝫ ordenauce/as for the hole brauche of the sayd acte ꝫ ord
naunce as fer as toucketh or concerneth these premysses be
ꝫ stonde auaillable ꝫ effectuell vnto thende of the sayd iiij.
yeres/ And from thende of the same iiij. yeres/ vnto thende
ꝫ terme of xx. yeres than nexte ensuyng/ Notwythstōdyn
ge ony acte ordpnaunce graunt or prouyso in this presente
parlement made or to be made/to ony marchaut straunger or
other/

Revocacion of kyng Richardis acte ayenst Italiens/

Itē the kyng our sayd souereyne lorde vnderstondyng
by a supplycacion put vnto his highnes in this his sayd
parliament by the marchauntes of Italye residente in this
his sayd reame of Englonde, that where by an acte of parle
mēte made in the parliament of Richarde late pretendynge
hym to be kynge of Englonde the thirde holden at Westmyn
ster the first yere of his reigne/it was ordepned ꝫ prouyded
that all marchauntes of the nacyon of Italie afore reherfed
not made denizenis whiche than had or shold haue wythin
this reame wares ꝫ marchandises broughte from beyonde
the see and byfore the fest of Ester than nexte ēsuyng shold
haue/shold doo selle or bartre theym in grose/and not by reta
ylle to the kyngis subgettis afore the firste daye of Maye

that thene sholde be in the yere of our lorde god M. CCCC
lxxvs./And the money comynge of the sale byfore the sayd
first daye wythin the same porte or portes where they arry
ued/ enploye vpon the comodytees & march andises of this
reame/theiz resonable costes & expenses allwaye except and
deducted vpon peyne of forfeiture of the value as well of al
the sayd wares & marchaudises kepte & not solde a fore the
sayd firste daye or otherwyse solde than is a boue sayd/ and
of soo moche money as sholde be made ouer by exchaunge con
trary to the sayd acte / And that all the sayd marchauntes
of Italy/the whiche after the sayd feste of Ester brought o
ny marchandyses or wares in to this reame to be solde shol
de selle or bartre the same wares & marchandyses in grose
and not by retayle vnto the kynges subgettes vpon peyne
of forfeiture of the value of the same wares & marchaudy
ses otherwyse solde/ And that the sayd marchauntes their
sayd wares & marchaudises whiche they sholde beyng after
the sayd fest of Ester shold woo bartre or selle the same with
in viii monethes nexte after their first arriual in to this re
ame in fourme a foresaid/and the money comyng of or bi þ
sayd sales or bartrynges of theim and eueri of theim enploy
and ther wyth bye the comoditees or marchaudises of thys
reame of englonde. wythin the sayd viii. monethes in the sa
me porte or portes where they shold first aryue/theiz resona
ble costes & expenses allwaye excepte & deducted . And that
they sholde in noo wyse make ony suche money ouer by ex
chaunge / And the sayd marchautes/ theyr sayd wares &
marchandyses remaynynge vnsolde/after thende of the sa
yd viii. monethes in no wyse sholde selle. nor bartre wythin
the sayd reame. but sholde cayre & conueye theym oute of the
same reame. wythin ij. monethes than nexte folowynge

14

after the sayd viij. monethes yf wynde and weder wyll se
ue it/And els as soone as wynde & weder wolde serue hem
after the sayd two monethes vpon peyne of forfeyture ai
well of as moche money as shold be made out of this said ti
ame by exchauge as of the sayd wares & marchadises soo
solde or bartred after thende of the sayd viij monethes not
carryed ne cóueyed out of this sayd reame/in fourme afore
sayd or the value therof the forfeitures penalte & losse of al
the premysses to renne & be vpon the said marchautes of J:
talie doyng contrarie to this acte/And also that noo straũ
ger of what coutrey so euer he were sholde oost or take to so
iourne with him wythin this reame of Englond ony mar
chaute straũger not beyng of the same nacion that he sholde
be of/vpon peyne to forfeyte & lose at euery tyme that he soo
dyde. xl li. And that noo marchaunte stranger sholde be at
ooste ne soiourne wyth ony other marchaut stranger not be
yng of his nacyon/or coutrey wythin the sayd reame vpon
peyne of. xl li And that noo straũger shold bie ony wolle
the whiche shold be sent or passe thrugh the streyttes of Mar
rok. by galayes or carekes or shyppes or other vesselles sor
ted clakked or barbed/Nor ony wolle wherof lockes or re
fuse shold be made/But that the same wolle/shold be as it we
re shorne & clene woude/wythout ony shoryyng barbynge or
clakkyng or lokes or refuse therof to be made. as it is afore
sayd. vpon peyne of forfeiture of the same woll/and the dou
ble value therof/as by the same acte more playnly map ap:
pere. Also that the sayd marchautes of Italy sholde haue &
cóueye their wolle wollencloth/and all other their marchan
dyses ouer the strettes of marrok. vpon peyne of forfeiture
of the same/as by the same acte playnly apereth/ The kyn
ge our sayd soucreyne lorde by thadupce of the lordes spyri:

tuell and temporell/and comens in this present parliamen
te assembled. and by auctorite of the same/hath ordeyned sta
blished and do to be enacted that the aboue sayd forfeitures
penaltees seisoures & actions comprised in the sayd actes &
euericke of hem. be reuoked voide annulled & of noo streng;
the agaynst all maner persones/excepte & reserued oonly to
the kyng/to be at libertye/ to haue & enioye all maner seiso;
ures forfeites & penaltees in the sayd actes specifyed. And
that it be liefull to the kyng to graunte to his sayd besechers
his lettres of saufconduyt & lettres patentes surely to be en
ioyed . accordyng to the tenours therof/ the abouesayd acte
& actes notwithstondyng/in as ample wyse as though thei
had neuer be had nor made/

¶ The seconde parliament holden the thirde yere of kyng
Henry the vij.

The kynge our souereyne lorde Henry by the grace
of god kynge of Englonde & of Fraunce & lord of
Irlonde the vij.at his parliamente holden at West:
mynst the ix.day of Nouembre in the thirde yere of his no:
ble reigne/To the worship of god & holy chirche/and for the
comen wele of this his reame / by thaduys & assente of the
lordes spirituell & temperell & the comens in the sayd parlia
ment assembled. and by auctorite of the same parliamente
hath ordeyned & established certeyn statutes & ordenaūces in
maner & fourme as here after ensueth/

¶ Yeuynge of lyuerey/& c̄.

¶ First the kyng our sayd souereyn lord/remēbreth how bi

Bnlawfull mayntenaunces gyuynges of liueres signes &
tokens & retoynoyes By endentures promyses other wrytin
ges or otherwyse/embrasaries of his subgettes Bn true demeanynges of shireffes in makynge of panelles & other
Bntrue retournes By takynge of money.By iurries.By grete
riottes & Bnlawfull assemblees . The police & good rule of
this reame is almost subdued/and for the nonn punyshyn
ge of thise ineouenyences/ and By occasion of the prompy-
ses noo 'kyng/or lityll maye be fonde By enquerry. Wherby
the lawes of the lond in execucion maye take lityll effecte
to thencres of mardres robberies periuries & Bnsuerties of
all men kuynge and losses of their londes & goodes/ to the
grete oysplesur of almyghty god / Therfore it is ordeyned
for reformacyon of the premysses by auctorite of the sayd
parliament/That the chaunceller & tresorer of Englonde for
the tyme beyng & keper of the kyngis priue seale. or ij. of the
ym/callyng to hym a bysshop & a temperall lord of the kyngis moost honorable couseyll. and the ij. chief iustices of y
kyngis bencke & comen place/for the tyme beyng. or other ij.
iustices in their absence/ Bpon Bylk or informacion put to
the sayd chauncell er for the kyng. or ony other agayn ony per
sone/for ony mysbehauyng afore rehersed. haue auctorite to
calle Byfore theym By wryt or priue senle.the sayd mysdoers
And theym & other By their descrecions By whom /the trouth may be knowen to examyn and suche as they fynde ther
in defectyf/to punysshe theym after their demerites/after the
fourme & effect of statutes therof made/in like maner & fourme as they sholde and ought to be punysshed.yf they were
therof conuycte. after the due ordre of the lawe/And ouer
that it is ordeyned By the auctoryte aforsayd/that the Justy
ces of the peas of euery shyre of this reame / for the tyme

kyng maye doo take by their dyscrecyon an enqueſt wherof
eueri man ſhall haue londes & tenementis to the yerely va
lue of xl. ſhelinges at the leeſt to enquere/ of the conceleme͂
tis of other enqueſtes taken afore thepm. and afore other of
ſuche materis & offences as ar to be enquerro/ and preſented
afore Juſtyces of peas/ wherof compleynte ſhall be made/ by
Bylle or Bylles/ aſwell wythin frauchiſe as withoute/ And
yf ony ſuche concelement be foūde of ony enqueſt as is afore rehersed/had or made wythin the yere/after the ſame conce
lement/ eueri perſone of the ſame enqueſt to be amerced for þ
ſame concelementis by dyſcrecyon of the ſame Juſtices of
the peas/the ſayd amerciamentes to be ſeſſed in pleyne ſeſſi-
ons   Item the kyng remembreth how murdres & ſleyng
of his ſubgettis daily encreſe in this lond/ thoccaſion wher
of be dyuerſe/ one that noo men in townes where ſuche mur
dres happe to falle and be doon/ wylle not attache the mur-
drer where the lawe of the londe is that if ony man be ſleyn
in the daye/and the felon not taken/ the townſhyp where the
deth or mudre is doon ſhall be amerced. And if ony man be
wouded in perill of deth. the partie that ſoo woudeth ſholde be
arreſt & put in ſuertie/ tyll parfyght knowlege be had wheder he ſoo hurte ſholde lyue or deye/ And the coroner vpon the
vieue/ of the body. &c. ſholde inquire of hym or thepm that
had doon that deth or murdre of their abettours & conſento-
urs/ And who were preſent whan the deth or murder was
doon whether man or woman/   And the names of thepm
that were preſente/ and ſoo founde to enrolle and certifye/
Whiche lawe by negligence is diſuſed. and therby grete
boldeneſſe is gyuen to ſleers and murdrers. And ouer this
it is vſed that wythin the yere & daye after ony deth or mur
dre hadde and doon/ the felon ſholde not be determyned at the

kyngis sute. for sauyng of the partie sute/ wherein the par
tie is oftymes slowe/ And also agreed wyth. and by then
ce of the pere. all is forgoten / Whiche is a nother occasyon
of murder/ And also he that wylle sue ony appele. moste sue
in propre persone whicke sute is longe/ and costely. that it
maketh the partie appellant wery to sue/ For reformacyon
of the premysses.   The kyng our souereyne lorde by thas
sent of the lordis spirytuell & temporell. and the comens in
the sayd parliament assembled/ and by auctorite of the same
wylle that euery coroner exercise & do his offyce. accordyng
to the lawe. as is afore rehersed/ And that yf ony man be
slayn or murdred. and therof the sleers murderers abletto
urs mayntenours & consortours of the same be endyted. that
the same sleers & murderers/ and all other accessories of the
same/ be arrayned and determyned of the same felonye and
murder at ony tyme at kyngis sute/ wythin the pere. after y
same felonye & murder doon/ and not tary. the pere & day/ for
ony appele to be taken for the same felony or murder. And
yf it happen ony persone named as pryncypall or accessorye
te be acquyted of ony suche murder/ at the kyngis sute. wyth
in the pere & daye/ that thenne the same Justyces afore who
me he is acquyted shall not suffre hym to goo at large/ but
eyther to remytte hym ayen to pryson/ or elles to lete hym to
baylle after theyr descrecyon tyll the pere and daye be passed
And yf it fortune that the same felons or murderers & ac
cessories soo arrayned. or ony of theym to be acquyte or the
pryncypall of the sayd felonye/ or ony of theym to be attem
ted/ the wyffe or nexte heyre/ to hym soo slayne as shall re
quyre maye take and haue theyr appele of the same deth &
murdre wythin the pere/ and daye after the same felonye &
murder doone ayenste the sayd persones soo arrayned and

                                                    B   iij

acquyte. And all other their accessories or apenst the accessories of the sayd pryncipall/or ony of theym soo attempted or apenst the sayd pryncypallis soo attempted / yf they ben on lyue. And the benefyce of his clergye. therof before not had. And that the appelaunte haue suche and like auauntage as yf the sayd acquytalle or attreyndre notwythstondyng. And ouer that the wyfe or kepte of the sayd person soo slayne or murdred/as case shall requyre maye comence theyr appell in propre persone/at ony tyme wythin the yere.after the sayd felony won before the shirref and coroners of the countie where the sayd felonye/and murder was won or before the kynge in his benche or Iustyces of Gayoll deliuerer/And the appellaunte in ony appelles of murder or deth of man where batell by the cours of the comen lawe/lieth not make theyr attourneys. and appere by the same/ in the sayd appelles/after they be commensed to the ende of the sute and execucyon of the same/And yf ony persone be slaine or murdred in the daye.And the murderer escape Bnta-ken/that the townshyp where the sayd dede is soo won be amerced for the sayd escape/ And that the coroner haue auctoryte to inquyre therof vpon the biewe of the body dede. And also iustyces of peas haue power to inquyre of suche escapes/and that to certifye afore the kynge in his benche/ And that after the felonye founde/the coroners delyuer the pr Inqupsicyons afore the iustyces of the nexte gayoll deliuerer in the shyre where inqupsicyon is taken the same iustyces to procede agaynste suche murderers yf they ben in the gayole.And elles the same Iustyces to put the sayd Inqupsicyons afore the kynge in his benche/ And for as moche as coroners had not nor oughte ony thynge to haue by the the lawe.for theyr offyce wyng / whiche ofte tymes hathe

ken the occasion that coroners haue ken remysse/ in doyng
their offyce   It is ordeyned that a coroner haue for his
fee.vpon euery inquisicyon taken vpon the vyewe of the bo
dy slayne .xiij. shelinges iiij. pens of the goodis and catal
les of hym/ that is the sleer and murderer yf he haue ony go
des/And yf he haue noo goodes/ thenne the coroner to ha
ue for his sayd fee/of suche amercyamentes as shall fortu
ne ony townshyp to be amersed for escape of suche murdre.
as is aforesayd/And yf ony coroner be remysse and make
not his inqupsicyons vpon the vyewe of the body dede/& cer
tifye it not accordynge as is afore ordeyned . that the coro
ner for eueri defaulte forseyte to the kynge.C.shelinges
And also it is ordeyned by the same auctorite / that euery
Justyce of peas wythin this reame/ that shall take ony re
conysaunce for the keppynge of the peas that the same Justi
ces do certifye/ sende or brynge the same reconysaunce atte
the neyte sessions of peas / where he is or haue ben Justyce
that the partye soo bounde.may be called And yf the partye
make defaulte.the same defaulte than there to be recorded
And the same reconysaunce wyth the recorde of the defaul
te be sente and certefyed in to the Chauncerie/ or afore the
kynge in his benche/or in to the kynges eschequer/

¶ Takynge of maydens/wedowes & wyues
    ayenste theyr wylle is made felonye /

¶ Item where wymmen as well maydens as wedowes
and wyues/hauynge substaunces /some in goodes mouabl
and some in londes and tenementes / and some keypnge ker
res apparaunt vnto their auncestours/ for the lucour of su
che substaunces ben often tymes taken.by mysdoers contrari
to theyr wylle/And after maryed to suche mysdoers or to

other by theyr assente. or deforced to the grete dysplesur of
god. and contrarie to the kynges lawes/and dispergement
of the sayd wymmen. and vtter reupnesse & dyscomforte of
their frendes. and to the euyll ensample of all other. It
is therfore ordeyned establisshed & enacted by our sayd souereyne lorde the kynge by thassente of the lordes spirituell &
temporell/and the comens in the sayd parliamente assembled. and by auctorite of the same/that what persone or persones fromhensforth that taketh ony woman so apenst hyr
wyll/vnlawfully. that is to saye. Mayde wydowe or wyfe
that suche takynge pwcurynge and abbettynge to the same
And also recepupnge wyllyngly the same woman soo taken apenste her wyll/ and knowynge the same. be felonye /
And that suche mysdoers takers & procuratours to the same . and recettours knowynge the sayd offence in fourme
aforsayd be hensforth reputed and iudged as pryncypall felons.   Prouyded allwaye that this acte extende not to o-
ny persone/takynge ony woman onely clamyng her as his
warde or bonde woman/

¶ Letyng to bayle of prisones arrested for light suspeccyon
¶ Item where in the parliamente late holden at westmynster the firste yere of Picharde late in dede/ and not in ryghte
kynge of Englonde the thirde/ It was ordeyned and enacted amonges other dyuerse actes/ that euery Justyce of the
peas in euery shyre cyte or towne shold haue auctorite and
power by his or their dyscrescyon to lete prisoners and persones arrested for lighte suspectyon of felonye in baylle or
maynprice. by colour wherof. afterwarde dyuerse persones suche as were not maynpreuable were often tymes letten to
baylle & maynpryse by iustyces of peas apenst the due fourme of the law/ wherby many felons escaped to the grete dis-
plesur of the kyng/and anoyaunce of his liege peple. wher

fore the kyng our said souereyn lord consideryng it by thad
uyse & assent of the lordes spirituell & temporel & the comēs
in the said parliament assembled. and by auctorite of the sa
me hath ordeyned established & enacted/that the iustyces of
the peas in euery shire / cyte & towne/or two of thepm at ÿ
leest wherof one be/of the quorū/ haue auctorite & power to
lett ony suche prysoners or persones maynpernable by the
lawe, that ben imprysoned wythin their seuerall couties ci
te or towne to baylle or maynprise . Bnto their nexte gene=
rall sessions/or Bnto the next gayolle deliuerer of the same
gayolles in eueri shire cite or towne/ aswell wythin frau
chies as wythout. Where ony suche gayolles ben or bere af=
ter shall be/And that the sayd iustyces of the peas or one
of thepm/soo takyng ony suche bayle or maynprise/ doo cer
tifie the same/at their nexte generall sessions of the peas/or
the next generall gailes deliuerance of ony suche gaile with
in eueri suche coutie cite or towne next folowyng.after ony
suche baylle or mainprise soo taken Bpon peyn to forfeyt Bn
to the kyng/for euery defaute ther Bpon recorded .p. li. And
ouer that it is enacted by the same auctorite/that eueri shi=
ref bayllif of frauchise.and euery other persone/hauyng au
torite/or power of kepyng of gaylis or of prisoners for se=
lonye/in like maner & fourme doo certifye the names of e=
ueri suche prisoner in their kepyng .& of euery prisoner to the
pm cōmytted for ony suche cause/at the nexte generall gay
le deliuerer in euery coutie or frauchies where ony suche gai
le or gaylles ben or herafter shall be/there to be calendred by=
fore the iustices of the deliuerauce of the same gayle. Wherby
they may aswell for the kyng as for ÿ partie procede to ma
ke deliuerauce of suche prisoners acordyng to the law Bpon
peyne to forfeyte Bnto the kyn ge for euery defawte them

recorded an hundred shylinges/ And that the forsayd acte
yeuynge auctoryte and power in the premysses to ony oon
Justice of the peas by hym selfe . be in that behalfe . Vtterly
voyde.and of none effecte by auctoryte of this presente par
liamente/

    ❧ Dedes of gyftes of goodes to thuse of the maker
       of suche gyfte be voyde/

    ❧ Item that where often tymes dedes of gyftes of goodes
& catalles/ben made to thentent to defraude their creditours
of their duties/And that persone or persones that maketh
the sayd dede of gyfte goeth to seyntuarie / or other places
preuyleged/and occupyeth & lyueth wyth the sayd goodes &
catalles / their credytours beyng vnpayed. It is ordeyned
enacted & stablisshed by thassent of the lordes spirituell & tem
porell/and at the requeste of the comens in the sayd parlia:
ment assembled ane by auctoryte of the same/that all dedes
of gyfte/of goodes & catalles made or to be made of trust. to
thuse of that persone or persones /that made the same dede of
gyfte be voyde.and of none effecte.

        ❧ Drye exchaunge

    ❧ Item for asmoche as importable domages losse & enpo
uerisshing of this reame.is had bi dampnable bargeyns gro
ued in Vsurie coloured by the name of newe cheuysaūce cō
trary to the lawe of naturell Justyce. to the comen hurte of
this londe.and to the grete displeasur of god /Our sayd so
uereyn lord the kyng for the reformacyon therof & of all co
rupt & diskfull bargeyns.by thassent of the lordis spirituel
& temporell and the comens in his sayd parliamente assem:
bled /and by auctoryte of the same hath ordeyned & enacted
that if herafter ony bargein couenaūt by byeng of ony obli:
gacion/bille or by ony pleges put for suerte. or bi bylle /or o
        ther wyse/

By the name of dyre eschaunge oz otherwyse wherby ony
certeyn some shall be loste by ony couenaunte or promesse
bytwyr ony person oz persones by theymself / oz ony other
to their knowlecke wythin this reame/oz yf ony bargein or
loue/wherby ony of the partie sholde lese· or paye for ony so
me certeyn, that is to saye / for hauyng a hūdred pounde in
money/oz marchandyse or otherwyse/And therfore to pay
oz fynde suertie to paye siy score poude, oz moze oz lesse/ in ҁ
for ony moze or lesse some after ony maner rate· that all su
che bargaynns couenauntes prompse ҁ suertyes therfore
made/and all thyng therof dependyng/ be vtterly boyde and
of none effecte/   And ouer this it is ordeyned by the sa̅
me auctorite/that yf ony marchandyses obligacyons byl·
les or plate be prompsed to be deliuered vpon suche corrupte
bargens and neuer deliuered or deliuered and had agayn
to hym that oughte suche marchaundyses/obligacions byl
les or plate/or knoweth by ony other man by assent aggre
mente/oz knowlecke in ony maner fourme l of hym oz his
factour oz broker that suche marchaundyses oughte·and oz
pryuee to suche bargeyns/that all suche bargeyns couenaū
tes prompses/and all suerties therfore made/be vtterly boy
de/And seller owner bargeyner or prompser of suche corup
te bargayns or goodes lease for ony suche bargeyn made/bi
hym oz his factour C.li. And whosoeuer wyll sue therfo·
re/ to haue an action of dette in whiche the partye shall not
wage his lawe· the kynge to haue the one half/and he that
wylle sue the other halfe.   And foz as moche as the·
se corrupte bargeyns ben moost vsuelly had wythin cytees
ҁ borughs /haupnge auctorite to trye alle materos ҁ causes
growen ҁ had wythin the same citees ҁ brughs·and if ony
suche defautes sholo there be tryed/peruryy by likilynes therby

sholde growe/and lytyll of the prempsses to be founde/Ther
fore it is ordeyned by the sayd auctoryte that aswell the cha
unceller of Englonde for the tyme beyng haue auctorite &
power to exampn almaner corrupte bargeyns prempses lo
nes or sales growen & had of ony of the prempsses/And
therupon by his exampnacion to here and determyne the sa
me/and to gyue like iugemente and make like execucyon
therof as the mater were tried & founde/at the parties sute/
in ony suche action of dette by the cours of the comyn lawe
as the iustyces of the peas of ony shyre next adioynyng to
ony cite or burgh where suche defautes be of ony of the pre
mpsses. And they to make like processe ageist ony man ther
of endited afore theym of ony of the prempsses.as they shol
de or owe to doo ageinst ony man that were indyted afore
theym of ony ryotte or trespasse.and to determyne it. And
yf ony man be founde gylty / afore theym of ony of the pre
mpsses to forfeyte the forsayd peyne of a hudred pounde. Pe
seruyng to the chirche / this punysshemente notwythston
dyng the correction of their soules acordyng to the lawes of
the same.

ℭ Eschaunge and rechauge

ℭ Item for asmoche as there hath growen/ & daily grow
eth grete dysplesur of god . and grete hurte of the kynge
our souereyn Lorde/ and to this his reame.By & for thynor
dynate chaunges & rechauges that haue ben of long tyme
vsed/and yet contynued in this sayd reame.wythout aucto
ryte gyuen of the kyng to suche chaungyng and rechaun
gynge ·   For remedy wherof many noble statutes
ageinst made .   Wherof one especiall statute made
in the fyftene yere of kynge Edwarde the thyrde

made for the same remedie · in Henry the fourth Henry
the v. and henry the sixthis dayes wherfore the kyng our sa
yd souereyn lord wylle. that all suche statutes be put in due
execucyon fromhensforth/ And that noo man make ony ex
chaunge without the kyngis licence. ne make ony exchaunge
or rechaunge. of money to be payed wythin this londe/ but
oonly but suche as the kyng shall depute therunto . to kepe
make & auswere suche exchaunges & rechaunges vpon the
peynes in the same statute of kynge Richarde conteyned/
And ouer that it is ordeyned by the kyng our souerepn lor
de by thassent of the lordis spirituell & temporell & comens
in his sayd parliament assembled / and by auctoryte of the
same/that all vnlefull chenysauncez & vsurie be dampned.
and none to be vsed vpon peyn of forfeyture of the value of
the money or goodes soo cheuesched or lent the same forfeitu
re to rene vpon the seller or lener therof ☾ Also for asmo:
che as dyuerse englishe brokers & estraungers brokers why:
che ben named & assigned to occuppe lefull broceage ben In:
ducers & bargayn makers of vnlefull chenysaunce & vsurie
and in some part of vnlefull exchaunges to the hurt of our
said souerepne lord & this his sayd reame. Therfor it is en
acted & stablished by þ sayd auctorite that all suche brokers
delyng vnlawfully/of ony of the prempsses be put a part
& neuer to ocupie as brokers within this his reame as thei
maye be aspied & foude in cytees burghs & townes.by may
res baylyffes or ony of thepm or of their mynystres where
suche bargen is vsed/ And that euery broker that is foun:
de defectyf.in makynge of vnlawfull brokage / shall for:
fepte/ for euery defaute yv. pound/ And haue enprysone
mente of halfe yere. And ferthermore to be punysshed by
the pilorie/or otherwyse to their opyn rebuke and shame.the

kyng to haue thone halfe/of euery of the sayd forfeytures
And the partie that wylle sue thother halfe/of the same by
action of dette/by the comen lawe/And the defendaut in the
same action be not admytted to his law ne esson ne protec
cyon be for the same defendaunt alowed/

¶ Concernyng custumers/

¶ Item the kyng our souereyne lord by thadupse & assent
of the lordis spirituell & temporell & the comens assembled
in his sayd parliament/and by auctorite of the same hathe
ordeyned & enacted, that euery marchaunt aswell denyszen
as stranger whiche shall bryng fromhensforth ony maner
of goodes in to ony port wythin this his reame by wey of
marchaudyse, and there do entre the sayd goodes or marcha
undises in the bokes of the custumers of the sayd port whe
re the goodes or marchaudises shall firste come to/And the
kyngis dutie therof to the said custumers contented or ther
fore with hym agreed/And afterwarde that doon wyll con
uey or carye the same goodes or marchaudises fromthens
in to ony other port wythin the sayd reame. That thene the
owner of the sayd goodes & marchaudises his factour or at
tourney shall bryng from the custumers of the porte where
the sayd goodes or marchaudises be soo entred a certifycat
vnder the same custumers seales direct to the custumers of
the porte wherunto the sayd goodes or marchaudises shall be
coueyed or caried makyng mencyon within the same certifi
cat aswell of the naturell colour length & value of all ma
ner of marchaudises so entred/vsed to be met wyth elne or
yerde as of the naturell weyght content or value of al ma
ner other marchaudises vsed to be wered or valued And y
the same certificat so made be deliuered to the said custumers
before the sayd goodes be discharged / soo that they maye see

whether the nature colour length/valure content or weyght
of the same/do agree/wyth the sayd certifycat/soo that the
kynge be not deceyued of his custumes & subsidies therof
due/And yf ony certifycat fromensfozth be made by ony cus
tumer of ony port wherвuto ony suche marchandises. or go
des shall be first brought vnto/and there in their bokes en=
tred/not makyng mencyon accordyng/as is afozsayd that
thene the said custumer or customers for their mysвyhaupn=
ge lose their offyce/and to make fyne with the kyng for the
same at his pleysur/ And ferthermore if ony suche goodes
or marchaüdyses or ony parcell therof be discharged vnpak
ked or put to sale wythin ony port than wythin the same
where they shall be first entred byfore the sayd certifycat be
delyuered / and the same goodes & marchaüdises seen accor=
dyng as a boue is expressed. That thene all the sayd goodes
oz marchaüdyses be forfeyted to the kyng our souerayn lord
thone halfe therof to remayne/to his highnes/and thother
half. to him oz theym whiche shall proue ony suche goodes or
marchaüdises soo forfeited. And that the custumer or cus=
tumers nor no deputie to ony suche comen officer / to whom
suche certifycat shall come/take noo thyng for the sight of
the same goodes soo certefied/ Also it is ozdeyned & stabli
shed by auctorite aforsaid/that noo maner of marchaüt de=
pnizen ne strauger do take vpon hym to do entre or cause
to be entred in the bokes of ony custumer of ony port with
in this reame/ony maner marchadises comyng in this his
sayd reame or goyng out of the same.in ony other marcha
üts name/Sauyng oonly the name of the true marchaüt
owner of the same/vpon peyn of forfeiture of al suche goodes
& marchaüdises so entred/And euery of the sayd marchaü
tes whiche so shal take vpo him to cause suche vntrue etre

to be made to haue prisonement and make fyne therfore/at
the kyngis pleasure/And that noo persone take vpon hym
to be customer coūtroller or serckeour in eny porte in ony cyte borugh or towne where he is comen offycer nor noo depu
te to ony suche comen officer vpon peyn of forfeiture for eue
ry halfe yere.that he occupyeth the sayd comen office & office of customership coūtroller or serckeour the some of xl.li.
thone halfe therof to the kyng/and thother half to hym that
wyll sue for it by wryte bylle or informacion)

Emploiement

¶ Item that where in the parliament of kyng Edwarde
the iiij holden at westmynster the vij. yere of his reygne/It
was ordeyned among other that euery marchaūt alien and
euery other viteler & other estraunger not beynge denyzein
that wsorte to ony place or porte wythin this reame or wa
les after the fest of Ester thene next folowyng sholde duely
enploye/all the money by hym to be wceyued wythin ony
porte wythin this reame or wales vpon the marchandyses
or other cōmodytees of this reame/or elles wythout fraude put the same money in due payment wythin this reame
the same enploiemēt or payment duely to be proued by the
marchāt viteler or other estranger byfore his departyng ou
te of the same porte by writyng fro that marchaūt or mar-
chaūter to whom the sayd marchaūt alien viteler or other es
trauger haue enploied or payed his money by hym wceyued for his marchaundyses brought in to this londe. Wyt-
nessynge that he hathe soo doon.or elles by suche proues as
shall be thought wsonable/to the customer or coūtroller of the
same portes or to the mayre baylyf or other chief gouerners
of ony cytie borugh or towne where suche port shall be.Vp
on peyne of forfeiture of all his goodes beyng wythin this

reame. and to haue enpryſonement of a pere ſauyng to eue
ry ſuche marchannt Vpteler ҩ other eſtrauger his reſonable
coſtes. Wpth certeyn prouyſions in the ſame. as by the ſame
acte more at large doth apere. Whiche acte was made to
endure/But oonly from the ſayd feſt of Eſter to the ende of
Vij. peres thene next ſuyng/ Soo that noo golde ҩ ſiluer re
ceyued by marchautes aliens ҩ other Vptelers ҩ eſtrangers
not beyng denizens for marchaudiſe brought in to this lõ
de is not employed vpon the comoditees of this londe. But
conueyed ҩ caried out of this reame to the grete loſſe to the
kyng. of his cuſtume ҩ ſubſidie/and enpouerſhyng of this
reame   It is enacted ordeyned ҩ eſtabliſhed by the kynge
our ſouereyn lord that now is/by thaduys of the lordis ſpi
rituell ҩ temporell/and at the prayer of the comens in this
ſaid parliament aſſembled/and by auctorite of the ſame/that
the ſayd acte made the ſayd xVij. pere of the reigne of kyn
ge Edward the iiij. Wyth all thynges compriſed in the ſa:
me/touchynge the prempſſes. and euery prouyſion made in
the ſame be good effectuell ҩ to endure for euer/ ¶ Alſo
it is enacted by the ſaid auctorite/that euery marchaut of Ir
relonde/Jerneſey or Garneſſey that bryngeth ony marchau
diſe in to this reame ſhall enploy the money receyued for the
ſame marchaudiſe. his reſonable exſpences deduct/ vpon the
comoditees of this londe/or elles Wythout fraude put the ſa
me money in due payment Wythin this reame/ The ſaid en
ployment or payment to be proued as is aforſayd/vpon pey
ne of forſepture of the Value of the marchaudiſe ſo brough
te in this londe. ¶ And it is ordeyned by the ſayd aucto:
rite that euery cuſtumer or coutroller ſhall take ſufficyente
ſuertie/for euery of the ſayd marchaut Viteler or other eſtra
unger to enploye. the Value of the ſayd marchaudiſes. or to

put the same monei for ẏ marchādise received in due paimēt
his resonable expences allwaye deducte. Vpon peyn of forfei
ture of the value/ of the sayd marchaudses. thone halfe of
the sayd forfeiture/ to the kyng/ thother halfe to the partye
that wylle sue/ This to begynne ⁊ take effecte at the fest of
Cristemasse nexte commyng/

¶ Apenst therdynauce of london of goyng to feyres/
¶ Item it was shewed vnto the kyng our sayd souereyn
lorde by a petityon put vnto hym/ in his sayd parliamente.
that how of late tyme/ the Mayre aldermen ⁊ citezeins of ẏ
citee of london/ haue made an ordenauce wythin the same ci
tee vpon a grete payn/ that noo man that is a free man or
citezein of the sayd citee/ shal go or come at ony feyre or mar
ket oute of the sayd citee of london with ony maner of wa
re or marchaudyse. to selle or to Barter/ to this entente/ that
all Byers ⁊ marchauntes shold resorte to the sayd cytee. to bie
their ware ⁊ marchaudyses of thesayd citezeins ⁊ free men
at london aforsayd/ by cause of theyr synguler lucre ⁊ avay
le. The kynge our souereyn lorde in consideracyon of the
hurt likly to growe. of ⁊ by the premysses. hath by the aduy
se ⁊ assent of the lordis spirytuell ⁊ temporell. and the comens in his sayd parliament assembled/ and by auctoryte
of the same. ordeyned stablisshed ⁊ enacted/ that euery free-
man ⁊ citezen of the sayd citee of london that now is or here
after shall be/ may lede carie ⁊ goo wyth his or their vytay
le ware or marchaudyse/ whatsoeuer it be/ at his or their li
bertee/ to ony fayre ⁊ market that shall please hym or theim
wythin this reame of Englonde. ony statute act or ordena
uce made or to be made wythin the sayd citee of london to the
contrarie of the premysses not wythstondyng. And the
sayd ordenauce ⁊ acte made in the said citee/ be voyde and of
none effecte/ And that noo persone of the sayd citee/ be hurte

nor preiudiſed in loſyng of his liberte & frauchiſe wythin ẏ
ſaid cite or otherwyſe By reaſon or occaſion of anullynge
of the ſaid ordenaunce and acte or for none obeyng to theſ
fecte of the ſame/ And pf ony perſone be preiudped in ony
wyſe. By occaſion of the ſame/that he that putteth or cauſeth
ony perſone to ſuche preiudpce/ looſe & forfepte to the kynge
p.li. as ofte as he ſoo doth/ And he that wyllt ſue for ſuche
forfepture/haue therfore an action of dette apenſt ſuche of=
fender/the kyng to haue epecucpon of thone halfe/ and he ẏ
ſueth thother halfe/ And in ſuche action the defendaunte be
not ampted to wagge his lawe .

    ℄ Domage geuen in a writ of errour
℄ Item that where often times plepntpf or demaudaunte
plepntfs demaundautes that haue iugement to recouere/ be
delaied of epecucpon for that the defendaunt or tenaut defen
dautes or tenautes apenſt whom iugement is gpuen. or o=
ther that ben bounde by the ſapd iugement/ ſueth a wrpt or
writtes of errour to adnulle & reuerſe/the ſapd iugement to
thentent oonlp to delap epecucpon of the ſapd iugement.
It is enacted ordepned & ſtabliſhed by thaduple of the lor=
dis ſpirituell & temporell. and at the praper of the comens
in the ſapd parliament aſſembled. and by auctorpte of the ſa
me/that pf ony ſuche defendaunt or tenaute defendautes or
tenautes/or pf ony other that ſhall be bounde/by the ſapd iu
gement ſue afore epecucpon hadde ony wrpt of errour to re=
uerſe onp ſuche iugement in delapng of epecucpon. that then
ne pf the ſame iugement be affermed good. in the ſapd writ
of errour & not erroneus or that the ſapd writ of errour be
dpſcontpnued in the defalwte of the pratie/ or that perſone
or perſones that ſueth wrpte or wrpttes of errour be
nounſued in the ſame that thenne the ſapd perſone or perſo=

nes apenſt whom/the ſayd writ of erwur is ſued ſhall reco
uere his coſtes & domage/for his delay and wrongfull ſey:
acpon in the ſame by deſcircion of the iuſtyce/ afore whom
the ſayd writ of erwur is ſued.

❡ Clothes to be caried ouer the ſee. be barked wſhed and
ſhorne excepte & c.

❡ Item where in the ſayd parliament it was ſhewed by the
remen fullers & other artifycers that ſholde liue and opteyn
their nedy ſuſtentacyon by meane of draperie/ made & dra;
ped wythin this reame. aſwell thorugh oute the ſame rea:
me. as wythin the cyte of london. that where as in a ſtatu:
te made the vij. yere of the reygne of kyng edwarde the iiij.
amonges other it is conteyned / that noo perſone denyzen
ne ſtraunger ſhold carie or doo to be caried to ony parties be;
yonde the ſee/ony woolen yerne/ nor cloth vnfulled. but the
woollen yerne to be made in this reame. ſholde be wouen in the
ſame/ And alſo all cloth in the ſame made. ſholde be fulled &
fully wroughte wythin this reame before that ony of the
ſame ſholde be had or caried oute of this reame vpon peyne
of forfeyture of the verey value of ſuche yerne/ not wouen
and clothe not fulled/had or caried oute of this reame/the
one halfe of the ſame forfeyture to be keyped to thuſe of the
kyng. and that other halfe of it/ to hym or theym that ſhold
eſpye or malie proue of ony ſuche yerne not wouen or clo:
the not fulled/caried to ony place beyonde the ſee/ And
for aſmoche as in the ſayd ſtatute of kyng Edwarde/there
is none expreſſe mencyon made that the ſayd clothes ſhold
be wſhed and ſhorne. afore that they be caried and conueid
oute of this reame/whereby the ſayd pouer comens of the
craftes aforeſayd myght be ſette in labour and occupacyon
therfore the ſayd clothes euer ſithen in to this daye/haue be

and yet daily arne. in grete nombre and plente carped & con
ueyed out of this reame vnwrowght and shorne/ in to the par
tie of beyonde the see/as well by denyzens as straungers
wherby oute londysshe nacions wyth the same drapery. arne
set in labour and ocupacion to their grete enrichyng/and the
pour comens of the craftes abouesaid/thrugh al this reame
that of naturell reason/as the kyngis true liege men shold
haue. & obtein their nedy sustentacon & leuing bi meanes of
the same draperi. for lacke of suche ocupacyon dayly fall. in
grete nombre. in to idelnes & pouerte/ to their vttermost dest
ruction. if it shold onylenger contynue The kyng our sayd
souerein lord the premysses considered. by thaduyse of the lor
des spirituell & temporell. and at the prayer of the comens in
his sayd parliament assembled & by auctorite of the same/
hath ordeined establisshed & enacted that noo straũger nor de
nizen carie or make to be caried out of this reame/ony wol
len clothes but that they before be barbed rowed & shorn wyth
in this same reame/ for the releef & settyng on werke of the
sayd pour comens/vpon the peyn & forfeyture limpted in the
said statute. of king edward/ made vpon clothes caried out
of this reame not fulled toke truided in maner & fourme as
in the same statute it is cõteyned/Prouyded alway that clo
thes called vesses rapes sapling clothes & all other clothes co
menly solde at xl. shelinges & vnder be not cõprised in thys
present acte/   ¶ Reteyndour
¶ Item the kyng remẽbryng how by the necligence & vn:
lawful demenynges of stuardes auditours receyuours sur
ueiours & baylifs of his honours lordshyps maners lõdis
& tenementis constables & kepers of castelles wardeins ma
isters of game & kepers of his forestis chaces parkes & wa
rens wythin this his reame grete vnsuertie hath growen

afore this tyme/aswell to his highnes/as to his progeny
tours. and how his tenauntes & inhabytantes of his sayd ho
noures lordshyps manoyrs londes & tenementes dayly ben
gretly troubled/aswell by thunlawfull retyners & retynew
es made aswell by the sayd officers. and suffryng the same
tenauntes & inhabitauntes to be vnlawfully retyned wyth
other persones/And how by this vnlawfull retynyng thei
ben called to vnlawfull assembles & riottes to their oft gre
te ieopdies & charges. wherby they ben soo enpouershed that
they ben not of power to pay to hym their duties. and his
subgettes nere their dwellyng ben beyed & troubled & gretly
hurt bi dyuers charges & vnlawfull imposicions/And o
uer this his highnes remembreth how his woodes his vert
& venyson by the wardeyns maysters of the game. parkes
kepers & other officers of his sayd forestes chaces parkes
& warens thrugh out this his reame. is almost destroyed
And that dyuers & many persones to whom he hath grau
ted suche offices in his grete troubles had ayenst his traito
urs & rebelles haue absented theym from his grace contrari
to the dutie of their alegeaunce & ayenst all trouth & kyndnes
Wherfore the kyng our souereyn lord wyll that. by thaduy
ce & assent of the lordis spirituell & teporell/and the comes
in this his sayd parliament assembled/ and by auctorite of
the same/it be ordeyned & enacted that if ony stuarde audito
ur recepuour suruepour or baylliff. that now is or hereafter
shall be/of ony of the said honours lordships manoyrs lo
des & tenementes constable or keper of ony of his sayd cas
telles/wardeyn mayster of game/parker keper or ony other
officer of ony of his sayd forestis chaces parkes or war
rens that now is or hereafter shall be/be vnlawfully retey
ned with ony persone/frohensforth. or retein ony man dwel

ling wythin ony of the sayd honours lordshipps maners lo
des & tenemetes. contrari to ony ordenauce or act afore this
tyme made/ or suffre ony man dwelling wythin the sayd ho
nours lordshipps maners londes & tenementis to be bnlaw
fully retepned wych ony other man or persone what degre
or condpcion soeuer he be of. And shelwe it not to the kynge
wythin xl dayes next after he hath knowleche therof. And
so w & with whom he is soo retepned/ Or ony of the sayd of
ficers couey ony of the sayd tenauntes inhabitauntes fermo
urs to the kyng/to ony felde or assemble or route otherwyse
than by the kyngis comaundement to doo hym suche serupse
as he shall be comauded/And that alway in the kyngis liuere or signe/wyth a conysauce of hym/that soo couey the
ym by the kyngps comaundement/Or pf suche offycer come
not to y kyngis highnes in tyme of trouble or werre/ wha
he therto shall be comauded hauyng noo resonable excuse/to
the contrarie/that all grauntes than made, or had to hym/of
ony of the sayd offices by the kyng/ or by ony of the kyngis progenytours or predecessours be thene Btterly voyde &
of none effect/ And it is ordepned by the same auctorite
that if ony fermour or tenaut wythin ony of the sayd hono
urs lordshipps maners londes & tenemetes be retepned with
ony persone or persones. contrarie to the statutes by liuere.
signe token or othe indenture or promyse/Or to goo to ony
felde gadryng or assemble .in ony manners liuere.signe or
token/But oonly in the kyngis liuere & signe . and to serue
hym oonly. or whexe he shall be comauded by the kyng/ that
all grauntes & leses to hym made for terme of yeres or at the
wylle/of londes tenementes rentes or other possessions beyng parcell of ony of the sayd honours lordshipps maners
londes & tenemetes/be thene Btterly voyde & of none effect/

¶ Item for asmoche as the grete and auncient defence of this reame hath stonde by tharchers & shooters in longbowes / whiche is now left & fallen in decay for the derth & excessiff price of longbowes / It is therfore ordeyned & establisshed by the kynge our soueteyn lord / by thaduys of the lordis spirituell & temporell & assent of the comens in the sayd parliament assembled / and by auctorite of the same. that yf ony persone or persones after the fest of the Purifycacyon of our lady nexte comyng selle ony longe bowe / ouer the price iij. shelinges iiij. that thene the seller or sellers of suche bowe forfeyt for euery bowe so solde ouer the sayd price vi. shilynges to the kyng. And he that wylle sue for the same haue an action of dette therfore, ayenst suche seller, or make informacion in the kyngis eschequer therof / the kyng to haue execucion of the moyte therof / and he that sueth thother moyte / And that in suche action of dette, the deffendant haue noo assoigne ne protection for hym alowed, / and he not admytted to wage his lawe /

¶ Felonye

¶ Item for asmoche as by quarelles made to suche as haue ben in grete auctorite office & of counceyll wyth kyngys of this reame / hath ensued the destruction of the kyngis & the neer vndoyng of this reame soo as it hath appered euydently. when compassyng of the deth of suche as were of the kyngis true subgettes was had / the destruccion of the prynce was ymagened therby. And for the most partie it hath growen & ben occasioned by enuye & malice of the kyngis owne howsholde seruauntes / as now late like thyng was likly to haue ensued / And for somoche as by the law of this londe yf actuell dedes be not had / there is noo remedye for suche false compassynges ymagynacions & confederacyes

had agayn ony lord or ony of the kyngis coūseill or ony of
the kynzis grete officers in his houshold, as stewarde treso
rer coūptroller. and so grete incōuenyences myght ensue of
suche vngoodly demeanyng sholde not be straitly punysshed/
or thactuel dede were don/ Therfore it is ordeyned by y̆ kin
ge the lordes spirituell & tēporel & the comens in the sayd par
liament assembled & by auctorite of the same/ that frō hensso
urthwarde/ the stewarde tresourer & coptroller of the kyngys
hous for the tyme being/ or one of theim haue full auctorite
& power to enquere. by vij. sad & discrete psones of the chek:
ker roll of the kyngis honourable housholde/ if ony seruaūt
admytted to be his seruaūt sworn & his name put in to the
chekker roll of his houshold whatsoeuer he be seruing in o2
ny maner office or romme. reputed had & take vnder the sta
te of a lord. make ony confederacies compassynges conspy:
racies ymagynacions wyth ony psone or persones to destro
ye or murdre the kynge or ony lord of this reame or ony o
ther persone sworn to the kyngis coūsepll/ stuwarde tresorer
coptroller of the kyngis hous/ that if it be foude/ afore the sa
yd stuarde. for the tyme beyng by the sayd vij. sad men. that o
ny suche of the kyngis seruaūtes as is aboue said/ hath cō
federed compassed comprised or ymagened/ as is aboue sayd
that he so foūze/ bi that enquerry/ be put therupon to answez
And the stuarde tresourer & comptroller or ij. of theim haue
power to detezmyne the same matez, accordyng to the lawe
And if he put hym in triell/ that thēne it be tried bi other vij
sad men of the same housholde. And that suche mysdoers ha
ue noo chalenge/ but for malice/ & if suche mysdoers be fo:
ūde gilty/ by confession or otherwyse. that the sayd offence be
iudged felony. And they to haue Iugement & execucion as
felons attempted owe to haue by the comen lawe/

¶ Cõspiratur

¶ Item for asmocke as afore tyme dyuerse persones feof/
offes of trust. and other whiche haue sued actions or sutes
to thuse of other persone or persones/and not to their vse ne
beboue haue be disabled to sue suche action or sute. And som
tyme barred in the same. by the reason that tho persones soo
suyng ben outlawed of treson felony or otherwyse/ Atteyn
ted coupeted or otherwyse dysabled to their grete delay & hur
te of thos persones to whos vse beboue & profyt the same ac/
cion or actions soo were sued or had. It is ordeyned esta/
blished & enacted by the kyng our souereyn lord/by thassent
of the lordis spirituell & temporell/and the comens in this
present parliament assemblead/ nd by auctorite of the same
that noo persone or persones whiche now hathe or herafter
shall haue ony action or sute hangyng. to thuse & beboue of
other persones than of theymself. be not fromhensforth dys/
abled ne excluded to pursue the same actions or sutes/and
execucion of the same to effecte by ony outlawry atteyndre
or conuyction/But that thoo persones soo suing may mayn
tene & pursue the same actions or sutes wyth lawfull exe/
cucions of the same. And thos persones to whos vse ony
suche thyng shall be recouered or had/ shal mowe haue and
enioye the same. the sayd outlawryes atteyndres or conuyc
tyons notwythstondyng / This acte to endure vnto the
next parliament.

To the worſhip of god and of all holy chirche/ And for the comen wele & profyt of this reame of Eng: lond/ Our ſouereyn lord Henry by the grace of god kyng of Englonde & of fraunce and lord of Irlonde the .vij. after the conqueſte at his parliament holden at weſtmynſter the .xiij. daye of Januarye/ in the fourth yere of his regne/ by thaduys & aſſent of the lordis ſpirituell & temporell/ and the comens in the ſayd parliament aſſembled/ and by aucto rite of the ſame/ hath won to be made ordeyned & ſtabliſhed dyuerſe ſtatutes & ordenaunces in fourme that foloweth.

¶ For commyſſyons of Sewers

¶ Firſt it was ſhewed by the comens in the ſayd parli ament aſſebled that where in the parliament of the right no ble prynce henry the .vj. late kyng of englond holden at weſt mynſter the .vj. yere of his regne, the conſidered grete hur: tes & loſſes which then were by theneueaſe of water in di uers parties of this reame / and many greter hurtes likly ſhold haue come yf remedye in that behalfe. ſhold not haſtly haue be purueyd/ It was enacted ordeyned & ſtabliſhed/ by auctorite of the ſame parliament. that for y. yeres than nex te folowyng. ſeuerall commyſſions of ſewers ſholde be made to dyuers perſones by the chaunceler of englond for the tyme kepyng. to be named in dyuerſe parties of this reame. where nede were. after the fourme & tenour of a commyſſion in the ſa id acte ſpecifyed/ And afterwarde in the parliament of the ſa id late kyng holden at weſtmynſter the .viij. yere of his reg ne/ by cauſe the commyſſioners named in the ſayd commyſſion had not playn power ne auctorite to do performe & exe cute thinges coprised in the ſaid commyſſion / It was ordey ned & ſtabliſhed bi thauctorite of the ſame parliamēt that al ſuche commyſſioners ſhold haue power to make & execute ſta tutes & ordenaunces after efect & purport of y ſaid commyſſion

And after the said x. yeres past in the parlyament of the sa
id late kyng/holden at westmynster the xviij. yere of his re/
igne. It was also ordeyned enacted & stablisshed by auctorite
of the same parliament/that for x. yeres than next folowyn
ge seuerall commyssions of sewers sholde be made to dyuerse
personea bi the chaunceler of englond for the tyme being/to be
named in all parties of this reame/where nede sholde be/af-
ter the sayd fourme & effect of the sayd commission conteyned
in the sayd act/made the said vj. yere/And that suche comis
sioners shold haue power to ordeyne & execute statutes & or
denaunces & other thynges do after theffect & purport of the
said commyssions/ And afterwarde in the parliament of the
said late kyng holden at westmynster the xxij. yere of his
regne/It was also ordeyned & acted & stablisshed/by auctori
te/of the same parliamet/that for xv. yeres than next folow
yng/the chaunceler of englond for the tyme beyng shold haue
power to make out of the chauncerie commyssions of sewers
vnder the grete seale /in suche fourme as it was graunted to
be made/by þ said act made/the sayd vj. yere/as in þ said act
is more playnly conteyned / And after the sayd xv. yeres
passed in the parliament of the noble prynce edwarde the fo
urth/late kyng of englond holden at westmynster the xij. ye
re of his regne/It was also ordeyned enacted & stablisshed/
by auctorite of the same parliament/that for xv. yeres than
next folowyng/seuerall commyssios of sewers shold be made
to dyuers psones bi the chaunceler of englond for the tyme be
ynge to be named in all parties of this reame & also of the
marches of calais guynes & hames where nede shold be after
the fourme & effect of the said commyssion conteyned in the said
acte/made in the said vj. yere . And that all suche commys-
sioners shold haue full power to make ordeyne and execute

ſtatutes ⁊ ordenaunces and other thynges to do after thef
fecte ⁊ purporte of the ſame cōmſſions/as in the ſame act
more pleynly is contepned/Bi which cōmſſions ⁊ auctori
te peuen to the ſaid cōmſſioners in the ſapd fourme many
grete hurtes ⁊ incōuenpeces in dpuerſe parties of this rea
me don ⁊ had Bi ēcreſe of water were neceſſarely redreſſed re
fourmed ⁊ amended/It is ſo now that late aſwell in the cō
ūties of gloceſtre ⁊ ſomerſet as elles where in dpuerſe partp
es of this reame.⁊ alſo wpthin the boudes of the ſapd mar;
ches of calaps gupſnes ⁊ hāmes/ By thencreaſe of waters
dpuers londes ⁊ tenementes in grete quantite ben ſuroūded
⁊ deſtroped/and many moo grete like hurtes ⁊ dōmages be
like wpthin ſhort tpme to fal/aſwell to the decreaſe ⁊ deſtruc
cpon of the liuelood of the kyng our ſouerepn lord as of the
liuelood of the chircke ⁊ of other true lige pepl of this reame
and of the ſapd marches ⁊ anpentiſment of the ſame.wpth;
out that remedpe in that behalf/be purueped ⁊ had/The kin
ge our ſapd ſouerepn lord therfore of his mooſt habūdanut
grace.the prempſſes tenderly conſideret bi thadupſe ⁊ aſſent
of the lordes ſpirituell ⁊ temporell/and at the requeſt of the
comens in the ſapd parliament aſſembled.and bp auctorpte
of the ſame parliament/hath ordepned enacted ⁊ ſtabliſſhed
that for poB.peres nept comyng ſeuerall comiſſions of ſelb
ers be made to dpuerſe perſones.bi the chaūceler of Englon
de for the tpme bepng to be named in all parties of this his
reame ⁊ of the ſapd marches where nede is or ſhall be. after
the fourme ⁊ effecte of the ſapd cōmſſion/contepned in the
ſapd acte made in the ſapd Bij.pere/   ¶ And ouer
that hath ordepned and ſtabliſſhed bp the ſapd auctorpte
that all ſuch Commſſponers haue full power to make
ordepne and epecute ſtatutes and ordenaunces and

other thynges do after theffecte & purport of the same compl
spon/ ❡ Fynours

❡ Item Where as it was of olde tyme vsed & contynued
tylk now of late yeres/that there was for the auayle of the
kyng & the wame fynours & parters of golde & siluer by fi
re & water vnder a rule & ordre/belonging vnto the myntes
of london/ calays/cauterberp, yorke, & durham, and in other
places where myntes were holden/ and at the goldsmythis
hall in london to fyne & part all golde & siluer belongyng or
nedefull for the sayd myntes & felishyp of goldsmythis for
thadmendemente of moneys & plate in the wame/that eue
ry thyng/myght be refourmed to the right standarde aswel
in moneys as plate. to the leest cost/for the wele of the kyn
gis noble men of the londe & comen prople. But soo it is
now/that suche fynours & parters of golde & siluer by fyre
& water/dwellen abrode in euery place of the reame, oute of
the rules aforsayd/and bie gylte siluer from the myntes cha
unges & goldsmythys. and parte & fyne it as is aforsayd
And for the moost parte/the siluer soo fyned. they doo alap
it in dyuerse maners, and selle it at their plepsure to euery
man that wylk bye it of theym/ to make suche werkes as
pleyseth the byers. Therfore men canne gete noo fyne siluer
whan they nede it/for their money/for thadmendemente of
money & plate as hath ben in tymes passed. Wherfore it cau
seth money & plate/in dyuerse places of the reame. to be
made werse in fynesse/than it shold be, as it appreth eupden
tly in diuers places to the grete hurt of y kingis noble men
of the londe & comen peple/Wherfore the kyng our said soue
rein lord/by thassent of the lordis spirituel & temporell and
comens in this sayd parliament assembled/& by auctorite of
the same, hath ordeyned establisshed and enacted / that noo

fynour of golde and siluer nor parter of the same/ By fyre
or water fromhensforth alaye ne fyne siluer nor golde nor
none selle in ony other wyse/ Ne to ony persone or persones
But oonly to thofficers of myntes chaunges & goldsmythis
wythin this reame. for augmentacion & amendyng of coyg
ne & plate as aforsayd/ And that the maysters of myntes
chaunges & godlsmythes for all suche fyne golde or siluer co
myng to theym. to answere the valour as it is worth acor
dyng as it is now & hath ben of aucient tyme accustomed
after the rate of fynes/ Ne that noo fynour nor fynours/
parter nor parters selle to no persone neyther to one ne to o-
ther ony maner of siluer in masse molton & alayed vpon pe
yn of forfepture of the same. the kyng therof to haue thone
halfe/and the fynder that can proue. and wyll sue it in the
kyngis eschequer thother half/And if ony fynour or fyno
urs parter or parters of golde & siluer either bi fire or water
alaye or selle ony fyne siluer or golde otherwyse than it is
ordeyned in this laste acte / be or they to leafe the valour of
the same golde or siluer soo alayed or solde/ the kynge therof to haue the one halfe. and the fynder that can proue it &
wylke sue it in the kynges eschequer the other halfe. Also
all suche fyne siluer as shall be parted & fyned/as is afore-
sayd/that it be made soo fyne. that it maye bere pn. peny we-
pght of alaye in a pounde wight/ and yet it be as good as
sterling and rather better than worse/And that every fyno
ur put his seuerall marke/vppon suche fyne syluer/ to bere
wytnesse to the same/ to be true as is aforesayd/ vpon the
peyne of the valure founde contrarye to be forfepte. the kyng
therof to haue thone half.and the fynder that can proue it &
will sue it in the eschequer thother halfe/ Also that noo
goldsmith

goldsmythis wythin this reame/ melt oz alay ony fyne sil
uer to ne for ony werkers or other entent/ but onely for ma
kyng of amelles for dyuerse werkes of goldsmythrie /and
for amendyng of plate to make it as good as sterlinge/or
better/for the comen wele of this reame (Nor that they selle
noo fyne siluer nor other siluer alayed molten in to masse/
to ony persone or persones whatsoeuer they be/nor one gold
smyth to a nother. This ordenaūce to be kept by the gold
smythis in euery poynt vpon peyn of forseyture of the sa=
me siluer or value therof/The kyng therof to haue the one
halfe / and the fynder that can proue it ℞ wyll sue it in the
kyngis eschequer thother half. ❡ Also it is ordeyned by
the same auctorite that all lettres patentes ℞ graūtes of of
fyces belongyng oz pertepynynge to the mynte of our souere
yn lord the kyng exercised in the same wyth fees ℞ wages
therto belongyng. be fromhensforth voide/℞ of none effecte /
                 ❡ Ayenst Bochers .

❡ Item it was shewed by a peticyon put to the kyng our
sayd souereyn lorde in the sayd parliameut by his subgettes
℞ paryshens of the parisshe of saynt Feythes ℞ saynt Gre=
gories in london nygh adioynaūt vnto the cathedrall chir
che of Powles/that it was soo that grete concourse of peo
ple aswell of hys riall persone/as of other grete lordes and
astates wyth other his true subgettes often tymes was
had vnto the sayd chathedrall chirche/and for the most par
te thorugh oute the parisshe aforesayd/ the whiche often ty=
mes ben gretly ennoyed ℞ inuenemed by corrupt eires enge
dred in the sayd parisshes by occasion of bloode ℞ other foul
ler thynges. by occasion of the slaughter of bestes ℞ scaldin
ge of swyne/had ℞ done in the bocherie/of seynt Nycholas
flesshamels /whos corrupcyon by violence/ of vnclene and

putrifyed waters is borne downe thrugh the sayd parisshes
and compasseth two partes of the palays where the kynges
moost ryall persone is wout to abyde. whan he cometh to þ
cathedrall chirche for ony acte there to be don to the Jubar-
douse abydyng of his moost noble persone/and to ouer grete ennoisaunce of the parisshens there. and of other the kyn
gis subgettis & straungers that passe by the same/ Comple
ynte wherof at dyuerse & many seasons almost by the space
of xvj. yeres contynuelly aswell by the chanons & pety cha
nons of the sayd cathedrall chirche/londlordes there/as al
so by many other dyuerse of the kyngis subgettes of righte
honest hauour vnto dyuerse maires & aldermen of the cite of
london hath be made/and noo remedie had ne foūden/that it
please our said souereyn lorde of his habūdant grace to pro
uyde for the conseruacyon aswell of his moost ryall perso-
ne/ as to socour his pour subgettes & suppliauntes in this
behalfe/ Consyderynge that in few noble citees and townes or none wythin cristendome. where as trauelling men
haue labored/that the comen slaughter hous of bestis sholde
be kept in ony speciall parte wythin the walles of the same
leest it myght engender siknesse. to the destruction of the pe-
ple/ The kyng our said souereyn lord in consideracyon of
the premysses/hath by thaduyse & assent of the lordes spiri
tuell & temporell/and the comens in the said parliament as
sebled. and by auctorite of the same. ordeyned and stablisshed
that noo bocher nor his seruaūt slee noo maner best wythin
the sayd house scalled the caldynge house. or wythin the wal
les of london. vpo ñ peyne to forfeyte for euery oxe vij. pens
and euery kowe & for euery other best viij. pens thone half
therof to the kyng our sayd souereyn lorde. and thother half
to euery of the kyngis lieges that wylle sue for the same/by

d   j

action of dette / And noo protection or essoyne be alowed to ony of the defendauntes agenst whom ony suche action shall be conceyued / And that in the same action of dette suche processe be made as in other actions of dette sued at the comen lawe / And ouer this it is ordeyned & enacted by the sayd auctorite that the same ordenauce acte & lawe extende & be obserued & kepte in euery citie burgh & towne walled wythin this reame of englonde / and in the towne of cambridge. the townes of berwyk & carlile oonly excepte & forprised. Prouyded alway that this present acte begyn & take effecte at the fest of anunciacyon of our lady nexte comynge and not afore /

¶ Protections for passers in to Bretayn

¶ Item the kynge our sayd souerayn lorde for dyuerse causes & resonable consideracyons hym mouyng / by thassent of the lordes spirituell & temporell & the comes in this present parliament assembled / and by auctorite of the same hath enacted ordeyned & stablisshed that euery persone of what condicyon or degree he be of / beyng or herafter be / in our sayd souerayn lorde the kyngis wages beyonde the see in Bretayn at his pleisure haue the protection of profecture or moratur cu clausula Volum9 / And in theyxcepcyon of the sayd protectyon there be made emyssion of assises. And that the sayd protection be alowable in all the kyngeys courtes / and other courtes where the sayd protections shall be pleded / or layd for ony of the sayd persones. in all pleys & assises. as well of nouell dissesin as of fresshe force / without ony dyfficultee. Also it is enacted that the iudgementes to be geuen fromthens forth in suche assise. arzained or to be arraygned shall not be preiudicyal to ony of the sayd persones soo beyng in the seruyse of our souerayn lord the. kyng. in Bretayn as is afore.

sayd whiche haue ony thyng in reuersion or remaynowe in
londes & tenemētes/wherof suche assise be arrayned/if the na
me of thos persones whiche ben in the reuersion or the rema
ynowe of suche londes & tenementes be not in the sayd assise
but that the sayd iugement be ayenst all theym. Boyde. The
sayd ordenaūce to endure & be auayllable/ to euery of the sa
yd psones as long as be abydeth soo in the kynges wages
And if this ordenaūce touchyng the sayd persones so now
abidynge/or that after this shall abyde/in the serupce of the
kyngis highnes in bretein be not sufficient for thease & su
ertie of theym/It is agreed & accorded by the same auctorite
That our sayd souereyn lorde the kyng & all the lordis of
his coūseyl for the tyme beyng/haue ful power in all maner
of actions sutes & processes to graūt to euery of suche perso
nes protection/as shall be in their cause auayllable after the
ir descrecyon duryng the tyme that they or ony of theym con
tynue in the sayd arme or warre/Prouyded that this act be
not auayllable to ony persone for ony entre sithen the firste
daye of this present parliament. Also it is enacted that yf
ony dyscent of ony londes or tenementes or ony other right
or hereditamētes be to ony persone or persones beyng wyth
in this reame or elles where/that that discent be of noo gre
ter effect to the dōmages or hurt of the sayd persones beyn
ge in the kyngis serupce/as is aforsayd. Thêne yf the said
persones in the kyngis serupse soo beyng were wythin the a
ge of xxj. yeres/ Also it is ordeyned by the sayd auctorite/
that all suche persones as shall passe ouer the see in the said
viage/and euery of theym whiche haue londes & tenemētes
holden of the kyng or of ony other shall mow lawfully ma
ke therof feoffementes & transmutacion of possessyon by de
de or dedes fyne or fynes recouere or recoueres for the perso

urmance of theyr wylles wythout ony fyne for the sayd fe
offement or transmutacion of possession therfore to be ma:
de in. And that they & euery of theym/ their heires & assygne
is of euery of theym be discharged of all suche fynes by the
sayd acte wythoute lettres patentes of licence/ or pardon or
other dyscharge to be had in that behalue. And ferdermo:
re it is also ordeyned & enacted by the sayd auctorite/that if
ony of the sayd persones soo passynge in the sayd byage
Whiche holde londes or tenementes of the kyng, or of ony
other by knyghtes seruyce or otherwyse, wherfore his hey:
re oweth to be in warde / and fortune in the sayd byage to
decesse/beyonde the see/ or that ony feoffement of the same lo
des & tenementes be supposed to be made by collusion, they:
re of the owner of the same londes and tenementes beyng
wythin age, that thenne the feoffes or executours of suche
persone soo deceased haue the warde & mariage of the heyre
soo beynge wythin age/ and of the londes & tenementes soo
holden duryng the nonage of euery suche heyre to the perfo:
urmance of the wylle of the sayd persone soo deceased with
out ony accompt or other thyng therfore to be pol den) Pro:
uyded allway/that if ony persone or persones reteyned in the
said arme or byage, resorte & come ayen in to this reame dis
charged of the said retenue armee & byage or after the said
byage determyned/that thene ony feoffement made by hym
or ony other to his vse of ony of the premysses be voyde &
of none effecte to exclude the kynge & his heyres or ony o:
ther for the warde & mariage/ of the heyre of ony of theym
soo comyng in to this reame by the vertue of this acte.

¶ Anullyng of lettres patentes made to ony spirituell
persone to be quytte for paymente of dysmes or for gade:
ryng of the same.

Item the kynge our souerayn lord remembreth both as
well his highnes as dyuers of his progenytours & predes-
cessours kynges of englonde, haue made & graunted vpon
feyned suggestyons to dyuers abbottes priours gardeyns
maysters or rulers of other spirituell places & to their successours dyuers & many lettres patentes / some of theym to
be quyt & dyscharged of gadryng of dismes / And some of
theym to be quyt & dyscharged of payment of dysmes / And
some of theim to be quyt & discharged aswel of the gadrinng
of dismes as of payment of dismes by the whiche euery dis
me whan someuer it be graunted / it is gretly mynyshed, and
other places the more greuously charged wyth the gadrinng
of the same / (Remembreth also the grete charges that now
ben in hande . and that the kepyng therof must aswell be to
the relefe of theym, that hath suche lettres patentes / as to o-
ther of his subgettes / Hath therfore ordeyned & enacted by
auctorite of the sayd parliamente . that all the sayd lettres
patentes / as for the premysses ben voyde / and of none effect
by what someuer names thos persones to whom the lettres
be made called or named /

Adnullyng of lettres patentes of ony offyce
in the forest of Ingelwood.

Item for asmoche as thrugh the necligence of stuardes
foresters & other kepers wythin the kyngis foreste of Ingle
wood in the shire of Comberlond, and by mysusing of their
offices . the dere & game is destroyed & goon bi occasion wher
of the sayd offyces requyren none actuell exercise. It is ther
fore ordeyned & enacted by auctorite of this said parliament
that all lettres patentes made by the kynge. our sayd souere
yn lorde of ony office wythin the sayd forest be from the first
day of this sayd parliament voyde & of none effect. Except

d.   iij

z/Prouyded that it be ordeyned by the sayd auctorite that the lettres patentes late made bi the kyng. to thomas lord dacre of thoffice of maister forster of the sayd forest stōd & be god de & effectuel to the same thomas after the tenour & effect of the same lettres patentes the sayd act not wythstōdyng. Prouyded also that this act extende not ne be preiudicyal to henry erle of Northhumbr. of or for ony graūt lettres patentes or confirmacōn made bi the kyng our souereyn lord to the sayd erle.   ¶ That all lettres patentes made to yomen of the corone. and gromes of the kyngis chambre/ for lacke of their attendaūce. be voyd /

¶ Item where dyuerse yomen of the corone & gromes of ꝑ kyng our sayd souereyn lordis chambre/haue dyuers offyces & fees graūted to theim/bi his lettres patentes for the cōsideracion of their attendaūce in the kyngis seruyce / whiche do nor endeuour not theymself. in yeuyng their attendaūce accordyng to their dutie/It is therfore ordeyned establisshed & enacted by thauctorite of the sayd parliamēt /that yf ony of the sayd yomen or gromes do nor yeue their attendaūce aboute the kyngis highnes accordyng to thordynaūce of his chambre. that thēne all lettres patentes to theym or ony of theym made or herafter to ony suche persone or persones to be made. be of no better force ne effect but at ꝑ kyngis plesure/

¶ Item for asmoche as drapers & taylours/and other in the cite of london & other places wythin this reame/that be sen to selle wollen clothe at retayll by the yerdis/sellen a yerde of clothe at excessiue price hauynge vnresonable lucre to the grete hurte and enpouershyng of the kynges liege peple byers of the same agenst equyte and good conscience. Wherfore it is ordeyned by the kynge our souereyne lorde by thad uyse of the lordes spirytuell and temporell/and the comens

in this sayd parliamente assembled/ and by auctorite of the
same. that noo persone selle wythin this reame at retaylle/a
brode yerde of wollen clothe of the fyneste makynge scarlet
grayned or other clothe grayned what colour soeuer it be to
ony of the kyngis subgettes aboue the price of xvj. shelinges. a brode yerde And a brode yerde of wollen cloth of ony
other colour oute of grayne. or ony maner russet of the fy-
nest not aboue the price of vj. shelinges vpon peyn to forfey
te for euery suche yerde solde to ony the kyngis subgettes a-
boue the sayd price xl. shelinges/ And of euery other clothe
what colour soo euer it be/ that is vnder the sayd price a bro
de yerde to be solde to the kyngis subgettes after the rate of
the goodnes therof/ And he that wyll sue for ony suche for
feyture haue an actyon of dette therof ayenst hym that soo
doth forfeite/ In whiche action none essoyn ne protection be
alowable/ And the defendaunt not to be admytted to wage his lawe/ The kyng to haue the execucion of the one halfe therof . and the partie that shall sue haue the other halfe/
This ordenaunce to begynne and take effecte from the feste of saynte Thomas the appostell/ In the yere of our lorde
god. M.CCCC.lxxxix. And the same ordenaunce befo
re the same feest wythin the sayd cyte to be proclamed/

℘ Price of hattes & bonettes
℘ Item that where afore this tyme it hath be dayly vsed
and yet is/ That certeyn craftemen named hatmakers and
capmakers doon selle their hattes and cappes at suche an
outerageous price/ that where an hatte stondeth not theym
in xvj. pens they wylle selle it for iij. shelinges or xl. pens
And also a cappe that stondeth not theym in xvj. pens/ they

d   iiij

wylle sell it for iiij shelinges. or v. shelinges.　And
by cause they knowe well that euery man muste occuppe
theym/they wylle selle theym at none esear price. to the gre=
te charge and dōmages of the kynges subgettes. and aga
ynst all good reason and conscyence　Wherfore it is ordei
ned enacted and stablisshed by the aduyse of the lordis spiri
tuell and temporell/and at the prayer of the comens in the
sayd parliamente assembled. and by auctorite of the same/
that noo hatter nor capper nor other persone selle nor put to
selle ony hatte to ony of the kyngis subgettes aboue the pri
ce of vp.pens the best/nor ony cappe aboue the price of ij she
linges viij.pens the beste at the moost/　And for all hattes
a cappes vnder the value to be solde at suche a price as the
byer and seller may resonable agree/　Vpon peyne of forfey=
ture for euery hatte or cappe otherwyse solde aboue the pry=
ce abouesaid vl.shelinges/　The one moyte therof to be to the
kynge our souereyne lorde/ and the other moyte to the par=
tie that wyll sue and proue the sayd forfeyture by action or
by actions of det by wryt at the comen lawe/ by.byll or pla=
ynt after the custume of cyte or towne where it shall fortu
ne suche forfeyture to be. in the whiche like processe Iuge=
mente and execucion shall be had as is vsed in actions bil
les or pleyntes of det sued/after the cours of the comen law
or custume of towne or cyte afore sayd/And that the defen
daunte in ony suche action bylles or pleyntes be not admyt
ted to wo his lawe.nor that ony protectyon or essoin therin
be alowed/This ordenaunce to begynne and take effect fro
the feest of saynt Thomas the apostle in the yere of our
de.M.CCCC.lpppip/ And the same ordenauce before the
same feste wythin the cite of london to be proclaymed/

　　¶ Of wyne a tolothse wode

¶ Item that where grete mynysshyng and decaye hath be now of late tyme of the nauye of this reame of Englond and pouerens of the marinens wythin the same / By the whiche this noble reame wythin short processe of tyme wythout reformacyon be had therin shall not be of habylyte ne power to defende it selfe / Wherfore the kyng our souerayne lorde. By thaduyse of the lordis spirituell & temporell / and at the praier of the comens in the said parliament assembled / and By auctorite of the same / hath ordeyned stablisshed & enacted that no maner of persone of what degre or condycyon that be be / conuey nor brynge in to this sayd reame / Irlond wales calays or the marches therof or Berwyk / from the fest of the Natiuyte of saynte John the baptist that shall be in the yere of our lorde god. M. CCCC. lxxxx. ony maner Wynes of the growynge of the duchie of Guyen or gascoyne or wood called Tolowse wode. but suche as shall be con ueyed anentred and broughte in shyp or shippes. Wherof our sayd souereyn lord or some of his subgettes of this reame of englond Irlond wales calays or berwycke ben owners possessours and proprietaries / And the maypster vnder god and the maryners of the same shyppe or shippes Englisshe irisshe or walshe or men of Berwyke or men of calays or of the marches of the same for the more partie. Vpon payne to forfeyt the same wynes and wood soo broughte contrary to this act / the one half therof to the kyng / and other halfe to him or theim that seasith the same wyne or wode / And also hath ordeyned and stablisshed by the sayd auctoryte that noo persone inhabyted wythin this reame other than mar chauntes straugers from the said fest of saynt John freight ne charge wythin this reame or wales ony shippe or other Vessel of ony alien or strauger with ony maner marchadise

to be caried oute of this reame or wales/ or to be brought
in to the same yf he maye haue sufficyente freight in shippes or vesselles of the denyzens of this reame in the same
porte where he shall make his freight/ Vpon peyne to forfei
te the same marchaundyses. the one halfe therof to the kyn
ge our soueryne lorde/ and the other halfe to hym or theym
whiche seaseth the same marchaundises/ ❡Prouyded
allwaye that this acte extende not to ony shyppe or shyppes,
hauyng ony of the said wares or marchaundyses constrey
ned by tempest of weder or enimyes to arryue in ony porte
or place wythin this reame/ Soo that the owners of the
sayd wares and marchaudyses make therof noo sale with
in this reame other thenne for vitaylle or repayryng of the
same shyppe or shyppes/ or takeling therof. whiche they of
necessitie be conpelled to make/

❡An acte vpon byeng of wolles ,

Item for the encrease and mayntenynge of drapery
and makynge of clothe wythin this londe/ The kynge our
soueryne lorde by the aduyse and assente of the lordys spiri
tuell and temporell/ and the comens in this presente parliament assembled/And by auctorite of the same hath ordey
ned establisshed and enacted/that noo maner of persone by
hym selfe/or by ony other bye or bargeyn from the fyrst day
of marche/that shall be in the yere of our lorde. M. CCCC
lxxxix ony wolles thenne vnshorne or take promyse of bar
geyne of ony wolles thenne vnshorne of the growyng of
Berkshire oxenfordshire gloucestreshyre herefordeshire shrop
shire wurcestreshire wiltesshire somersetshire dorsetshire hap
shire essex hertfordeshire cambrydge north. suff. kente surrey g

suffer / or ony of theym afore the feest of the Assumpcyon
of our lady thenne nexte ensuyng. or bye or bargeyne ony
wolles or take promyse of bargeyn of ony wolles that shal
growe in ony of the same shyris in ony yere or yeres to co
me after the said fest of Assumpcion of our lady ony tyme
before the same feste of assupcion of our lady that shall be
nexte after the sherpng of the same wolle or wolles / But
oonly suche persones as of the sayd wolles shall make or
doo to be made yerne or cloth wythin this reame. Vpon peyn
of forfeyture of the double value of all the wolles broughte
or to be bargeyned or taken by promyse of bargeyn contrary
to this ordenauce / Nor that ony marchaunt straunger by
hymself or by ony other persone in ony yere to come bye ony
wolles before the feest of the purifycacion of our lady nex
te after the cleppyng or sherpng of the same Vpon like pyn
of forfeyture /   The one halfe of suche forfeyture to be had
to the kyngis Vse. And the other halfe therof to the Vse of
hym that wylle sue the partie that soo shall brake the sayd
ordenauce / And that ony persone that wyll sue in that par
tie / haue an action of dette of the forsayd forfeyture and su
che processe in the same action to be had. as is in an actyon
of dette at the comen law / or after the custome of the cyte bo
rugh or towne / Where it shall hap to be sued. And that noo
essoyn ne protection be alowed for the offendaut in that ac
tyon / nor that the sayd offendaunt therin be admytted to
wage his lawe .   ¶ It is also ordeyned by the sayd auc
torite that noo maner persone beynge sworne to be a wolle
packer in ony wyse / after the sayd first daye of Marche / bie
bargeyn ony maner wolle for ony suche marchaut strauger
wythin this reame Vpon pyne of forfeyture of the same
wolle soo boughte bargeyned, or gadred to the Vse of

ony suche marchaunt stranger/ This ordena unce to endure
from the sayd first daye of marche Vnto thende & terme of x
yeres thêne next ensuyng.

¶ Actus sup pclam

¶ Item the kyng our souereyn lord considereth that by the
necligence mysdemeanyng fauour & other inordinat causes
of the iustices of peas in euery shire of this his reame / the
lawes & ordenaûces made for the politique wele peas & gode
rule of the same. and for the profit suerte & vsefull lyuyng
of his subgettes of the same be not duely executed accordin
ge to the tenour & effecte that they were made & ordeyned for.
Wherfore his subgettes ben greuously hurt/and out of sure
tie of their bodies & goodes to his grete dyspleysure/ for to
hym is noo thyng more iopous thêne to knowe his subget
tes to liue peasible Vnder his lawes. and to encrease in wel
the & prosperite/ And to avoyde suche enormytes & inuries
soo that his sayd subgettes maye liue vestfull Vnder his pe
as & lawes to their encrease/ He wyll that it be ordeyned & e
acted by thauctorite of this present parliamêt y euen iustice
of peas wythin euery shire of this his sayd reame wythin
the shire where he is iustice of peas/do cause openly & solêp
ly to be proclaymed yerely/iiij. tymes in a yere. in iiij. pryn
cipall sessions the tenour of this proclamacyon to this byll
anneyed. And that euery iustyce of peas beyng present at o
ny of the sayd sessions yf they cause not the sayd proclamacy
on to be made in fourme aboue sayd/ shall forfeyte to our sa
id soueyn lord at euery tyme xx. shelinges

¶ De pclamacôe facienda.

¶ Henricus dei gra & c/ The kynge our souereyne lorde
considereth howe dayly wythin this reame his coyne is trap
tourlly counterfeyted murders robberyes felonyes ben

greuouslp commytteo and won. And also Bnlawfull retey
uers pokenesse Bnlafull plepes extorsions mysdemenynges
of Shirueffes ercketours. and many other enormytes ¶ Bn
lawful demenynges daily growpth/ And more sith within
this his reame to the grete dyspleyʃure of god hurt ¶ enpo
uershpng of his ʃubgettes/ and to the ʃubuercion of the po
secie ¶ goode gouernaunce of this his reame/ For by thyʃe
ʃapd enormytees ¶ myʃchfes his pea is broken/ his ʃub
gettes troubled inqupeted ¶ impouershed. the houʃbondrie of
this londe decaped/ Wherby the chirck of englonde is Bphol
den/ the ʃerupce of god contpnued. euery man therby hathe
ʃuʃtenaunce euery enheritour his rente for his londe/ For
repreʃʃhpnge and auopdpng of the ʃapd myʃchefes ʃuffpci
ente lawes and ordenaunces ken made by auctorpte of ma
np and dpuerʃe parliamentes holden wpthin this reame to
the grete coʃte of the kpng his lordis and comens of the ʃa
me/ And lacketh noo thpnge/ But that the ʃapd lawes ken
not put in due epecucion. Whiche lawes ought to ke put in
due epecucion by the Juʃtice of peas in euery ʃhpre of this
reame. to whom his grace hath put and gpuen full auctorp
te ʃoo to wo ʃpth the kegpnnpng of his repgne. And now
it is comen to his knowlkage that his ʃubgettes ke litell ea
ʃed of the ʃapd myʃchefes by the ʃapd iuʃtpces. But by many
of thpm rather hurte than helped. And if his ʃubgettes cō
plapn to thiʃe Juʃtices of peas of onp wronges won to the
pm/ they haue therby noo remedp/ And the ʃapd myʃchfes
wo encreaʃe. and not ʃubdued. And his grace conʃidereth
that a grete part of the welth ¶ proʃperite of this londe ʃtan
deth in that/ that his ʃubgettes map liue in ʃuerte Bnder his
peas in their kodies ¶ goodes/ And that the huʃbondrp of
this londe mape encreaʃe/ and ke Bpholden/ Whpche muʃte

shall gyue hym a daie by his discrescion to brpng in his sa
yd lettres or certifycat/And yf he fayle and bryng not in at
suche a daye his sayd lettres nor certifycat/thenne the same
persone to lose the benefyce of his clergy.as he shall do that
is wythout orders.

¶ Adnullyng of the seale of therldome of Marche
¶ Item where afore in the tyme of kyng edwarde the iiij
all feoffementes gyftes grauntes dyuerse presentementes
nomynacions releaces warrauntes & confirmaciōs made to
ony persone or persones of ony castelles honours manoyrs
londes & tenementes or other heredytamentes or auaunta
ges percell or pertepnyng to therldome of marche. Or pertey
npng to ony maners londes or tenementes/ and other here
dytamentes in demesue.or reuersion percell/ or pertepnynge
to the sayd erldom of marche were made & passed bnder a spe
ciall seale named the seale of the marches. Wherby is grow
en grete separacion/trouble & dysceyte of the subgettes of the
kyng our souereyne lorde. Wherfore it is enacted by thauc
torite of this present parliament/that all feoffementes gyf
tes grauntes dymises presentementes nompnacyons/and
all other wrytynges.Wherto sealing is requysite to be made
After the fest of the purifycacion of our lady in the b.yere
of the regne of our souerepn lorde that now is.of ony par
cell of the sayd erledome be had done & made by the kyng our
sayd souereyne lorde/bnder the brode seale of his chauncery
as it is bsed in all other thynges/concernynge the crowne/
by the cours of the comen lawe/and by none other seale.

¶ For the Mayre of London
¶ Item where the maire of the cite of london for the tyme
beyng.is conseruatour hauyng the conseruacie of the water
and ryuer of thampe from the brydge of Stapns bnto the

waters of yendale & medewaye/ It is soo that wythin fewe
yeres by tempeste of weder & grete habundance of waters in
the said ryuer of thampse, diuers brockes issues & crekes ha
ue ben & growen oute of the sayd ryuer of thampse. And bi
the same dyuers pastures medowes & groundes of dyuerse
persones ben drowned & ouerflowen/ In whiche brockes issu
es & crekes & grounde drowned, the frie & brode of fisshe for
the moost parte restith. and in the same places the sayd frie
& brode in grete multitude ben dayly taken by the sayd fys=
shers there wyth vnlawfull engynes & nettes for bayte of
elis & coddys. And also for fedyng of their hogges to thut
ter destruction of the sayd frie & brode/ wythout a remedy the
rather be prouyded/ The kyng our sayd souereyn lord by the
aduyse & assent of the lordes spirituell & temporell/and atte
the prayer of the sayd comens in the sayd parliament assem
bled.and by thauctorite of the same.hath ordeyned establis=
shed & enacted/ that the Mayer of london & his successours
maires for the tyme beyng haue the conseruacy & rule & like
auctorite in euery of the sayd brockes issues & crekes & gro=
ude soo drowned.and ouer flowen as ferre as the water eb=
beth & flowyth as towchyng the punycyon for vsing of vn
lawfull nettis & other vnlawfull engynes in fysshyng li=
ke as he & his predecessours haue had or hath in the same
water & ryuer of thampse. wythin the bondes afore rehersed/
And to doo all other like correction & punysshements them
concernyng the reformacion and redresse of vnlawfull net
tes & engines/as he & his predecessours haue vsed & owe to
vse in the sayd ryuer of thampse. le Roi le vuelt/ ¶ Pro=
uyded allway that the mayre of london nor his successours
maires for the tyme beyng/ haue not the conseruacion nor
rule ne auctorite in ony of the sayd brockes issnes crekes &

gwundes so drowned.and ouerflowen wythin the kyngis
gwunde or beyng wythin ony frauchises of ony persone or
persones spirytuell or temporell/ as touchyng the punyci
on for vsing of vnlawfull nettes ꝗ other vnlawfull engy
nes in fysshyng nor to doo ony correction or punysshmēt the
re concernyng the reformacion ꝗ redresse of vnlawfull net
tes ꝗ engynes / as the sayd mayre ꝗ his predecessours haue
vsed.and owe to vse in the sayd ryuer of Thamys

The Ile de Wyght

¶ Item for asmocke as it is to the kyng our souerayn lor
de grete suerte/and also to the suerte of the reame of englon
de.that the Ile of Wyght in the coūtie of Sutht be well in
habited with englisshe peple for the defense aswell of his aū
cient empes of the reame of fraūce/as of other parties/The
whiche ile is latly decaied of peple by reason that many tow
nes ꝗ vyllages ben sete downe. and the feldes diched ꝗ made
pastures for bestes ꝗ catelles. And also many dwellyng
places fermes ꝗ fermeholdes haue of late tyme be vsed to be
taken in to one mānys holde ꝗ handes/that of olde tyme we
re wonte to be in many seuerall persones holdes ꝗ handes/
and many seueral housholdes kept in theym.And therby mo
che peple multiplied / and the same Ile therby well inhabited
the whiche now by thoccasion aforsayd is desolate / and not
inhabyted/but ocupyed wyth bestes ꝗ catelles.Soo that yf
hasty remedy be not prouyded. that ile can not be long kept
ꝗ defended/but open ꝗ redy to thandes of the kyngis empes/
whiche god forbede/ For remedie wherof it is ordeyned en
acted ꝗ stablysshed by thaduyse ꝗ assent of the lordes spiritu
ell ꝗ temporell.and the comens in this present parliamente
assembled/and by auctorite of the same. that fromhensforth
noo maner of persone of what estate degre or condycion be

is or shall be/ take ony seuerall fermes moo thenne one. of
maners londes & tenemetes persfonages or tithes wythin the
sayd ile. Wherof the ferme of thepm all togeder shall exceed y
some of y.marke perely/And yf ony seueral lefes afore this
tyme haue ben made/ to ony perfone or perfones of dyuerfe
sudzi fermeholdes ouer the faid perely value of y.make the͂:
ne the perfone oz perfones that now holde the fame. to chefe
one or moo of the faid fermeholdes at his pleifuz/Soo that
the ferme of thepm all foo chofen be not aboue the perely va:
lue of y.marke to holde after the fourme of his lees/and the
remnaut from the feft of faynt mychell tharchangel whiche
shall be in the pere of our lorde M.CCCC.lxxxx.to ceafe
& be vtterly voyde/And the ocupier & termer of thepm from
thens to be dyfcharged ayenft his leffour of the rent refer:
ued vpon the fame leefes/And yf ony perfone doo here after
the contrare of this act/ that thene the leeffe in that behalfe
forfeyt to the kyng for euery fuche takyng x.li. Prouyded
allwayes that they whiche haue payed ony fynes or made o
ny byldyng or done grete reparacion vpon ony fuche ferme
and be put from the fayd ferme by reafon of this act shal be
recompenfed for fuche byldyng oz reparacion as right & good
confcience requyren/that recompence to be adiudged bi the dif
crecion of the capitayne of the fayd ile/foz the tyme beynge
or his lieftenaut of the fame in his abfence/

      ❡ Wardes

❡ Item Where by an eftatute made at marlebridge/ It
was ordeyned p whan tenautes made feoffemetes in frau:
de to make the lordes of the fee. to lefe their wardes/The lor
des sholde haue writtes to recouer their wardes ayenft fuche
feoffes as in the fayd eftatute amonge other thynges appe
reth more plepnly atte large/Syth the makynge of whiche

eſtatute many pmagynacions haue ben had ⁊ yet ben vſed
as well by feoffementes fynes ⁊ recoueres as otherwiſe/ to
put lordes from theyr wardes of londes holden of theym by
knyghtes ſeruyce. It is therfore ordeyned eſtabliſhed ⁊ enac
ted by auctorite of the ſaid preſent parliamēt· that ꝑ ſaid eſ
tatute of markeburgh be obſerued ⁊ kept in al maner of thin
ges after the fourme ⁊ effect therof/ And ouer that it is or
deyned ⁊ enacted bi the ſaid auctorite that yf ony perſone or
perſones of what eſtate degree or condicyon be or they be of
or bere after ſhall be/ſeyſed in demeane or in reuerſion of eſ
tate of heritauce beyng tenaūt immediat to the lordis of ony
caſtelles maners londes ⁊ tenemētes or other hereditamen
tes holden by knyghtes ſeruyce. in his or their demeane/ as
of fee. to thuſe of ony other perſone or perſones ⁊ of his bey
res onely. be to whos vſe. he or they be ſo ſeiſed dieth his hey
re beyng wythin age / noo wylle by hym declared nor made
in his lif. touchyng the prēmyſſes or ony of theym/ The lor
de of whom ſuche caſtelles maners londes tenementes ⁊ he
redytamētes ben holden immediatly ſhal haue a writ of riht
of warde as well for body as for the londe/as the lord ſholde
haue had yf the ſame auceſtre had be in poſſeſſion of that eſ
tate. ſoo beyng in vſe at tyme of his deth · ⁊ noo ſuche ſtate
to his vſe made / And yf ony ſuche heire be of full age. at ꝑ
deth of his auceſtre to pay a relef as his auceſtre whos hey
re he is had be in poſſeſſion of that eſtate ſoo beyng in vſe
at tyme of his deth/ and no ſuche eſtate to his vſe made nor
had. It is alſo ſtabliſhed ⁊ enacted by the ſaid auctorite. that
ſuche heire or heyres ſo beyng in warde ſhal haue like action
of waſt apēſt the ſaid lordis or ayenſt theym in whos war
de they ſo be as they or ony of theym ſhold haue had/and re
couere ſuche domages ⁊ ſuche penalties to be to the ſaid lord

and gardeyns as sholde haue ben if their auncestres had dei
ed therof. seised/ And ouer yf ony suche lorde bryng ony su
che wrpt of right of warde ayenst suche persone or persones
and be barred in the same that thenne the same deffendaunt
or defendautes shall recouer damages ayenst the sayd plein
tifs for their wrongfull vexacion in the same/ Prouyded
allwayes that this acte/ begyn to take effecte of theyres of
thepm that shal deye after the fest of Ester that shall be in
the yere of our lord M.CCCC.lxxxx.

℄ Forgynge & coūtrefeytyng of golde & siluer of other
londes suffred to renne in this reame is made treyson/

℄ Item for asmocke as by the kyngis sufferauce/ dy:
uers coigne of golde & siluer. Whiche be not of the kingis pro
per coygne of englonde be currante in payment wythin this
reame dyuers & many euyll disposed prisones perceyuyng y
the forgyng & coūtrefeytyng of suche coygnes is nether felo
ny nor treyson/ presume & take vpon thepm for their syngu
ler auayle & profyte to coūtrefeyt & forge suche coynes/ to the
grete hurte & preiudyce/ aswell of the kyng our souerepn lor
de as to the hurte of all the kyngis subgettes It is therfo
re ordeyned & stablisshed by auctorite of the sayd parliament
that the coūtrefeytyng & forgyng of euery suche coyne/ be ad
iuged treyson. as it is of the coūtrefeytyng of the propre coi
ne of the kyng of this reame/

℄ For keppyng vp of houses for husbondrye

℄ Item the kynge our souerepn lorde hauynge a singuler
plepsur aboue all thynge to auoyde suche enormytees & mys
cheuous. as ben hurtful & preiudyciall to the comen wele of
this his lande and his subgettes of the same/ Remembreth
that amonge all other thynges grete incōuenyences/ dayly
wo encrease by desolacion and pullyng downe and wylfull

d iij

waſt of houſes and townes wythin this his reame/and ke
ping to paſture londes whiche cuſtumably haue ben vſed in
tylthe. wherby poleneſſe is growde and begynnyng of all myſ
cheuous dayly doth encreaſe/For where in ſome townes ij
hundred perſones were occupyed & liued by their lawfull
labours. now ben there occupyed ij.or iij.herdmen/ and the
reſidue falle in ydlenes/the huſbondrie whiche is one of the
grettest comodities of this reame is gretly decayed/churches
deſtroyed / the ſeruyſe of god wythdrawen/ the bodies there
beried not praied for/The patrone & curates wronged, the de
fenſe of this londe ayenſt our enimyes outwarde febled and
impayred/to the grete diſpleyſur of god. to the ſubuerſion of
the policie & good rule of this londe/and remedy be not ther
fore haſtly purueyed/Wherfore the kyng our ſayd ſouerein
lorde. by thaduyſe of the lordes ſpirituell & temporel/and the
comens in the ſayd parliament aſſembled. and by auctorite
of the ſame hath ordeyned enacted & ſtabliſhed that noo per
ſone what eſtate degree or condicyon that he be/that hath o
ny hous or houſes that at ony tyme within iij.yeres paſſed
hath ben or that now is or herafter ſhal be/ leten for ferme
wyth xx.acres of londe at leeſt or more/lyinge in tyllage &
huſbondrie/that the owner or owners of eueri ſucke houſe
or houſes & londe. be bounde to kepe ſuſteyn & mayntene hou
ſes & byldynges vpon the ſayd grounde & londe conuenyent
& neceſſarie for mayntenyng & vpholdyng of the ſayd tyllage & huſbondrie/And yf ony ſucke owner or owners of o-
ny ſucke houſe or houſes & londe take kepe & occupye ony ſu
cke hous or houſes & londe in his or their owne handes that
the ſayd owner or owners by the ſayd auctorite be bounde/
in like wyſe to kepe & mayntene houſes & byldynges vpon y
ſayd grounde & londe conuenyent & neceſſary for y mayntening

& vpholdyng of the sayd tillage & husbondrie / And yf ony
man soo contrarie to the prempsses or ony of theim, that
thenne it be liefull to the kyng/ yf ony suche londes or hou=
ses be holden of hym.immedyatly/or to the lordes of the fees
yf ony suche londes ben holden of theym/immediatly to recei
ue yerely halfe the value of thyssues & profytes of ony su=
che londes. wherof the house or hou[s]es ben not soo maynteened
& sustepned / And the same halfendele of thissue & profytes
to haue holde & kepe to his or their owen vse/wythoute ony
thyng therfore to be payed or peuen.to suche tyme as the sa
me house or houses be suffyciently bylded or repayred vpen
And that noo maner of freholde be in the king ne in ony su
che lord or lordes by the takyng of ony suche profytes of or
in ony suche londes in noo maner of fourme But oonly the
kyng/And the sayd lord or lordes haue power to take recei
ue & haue the sayd yssues & profytes as is aboue sayd/And
therfore the kyng .or the sayd lord or lordes to haue power
to dystreyne for the same/issues & profytes to be had & percey
ued by theym/in fourme aboue sayd by auctorite of this pre
sente acte/

¶ Actions populers

¶ Item that where actions populers in dyuerse causes ha
ue ben ordeyned bi many good actes & statutes afore this ti
me made for the reformacion of extorsious mayntenaunce op
pressions Iniuries exactions & wronges vsed & compterd
wythin this reame/ whiche actions ben very penall to alle
mysdoers & offendars in suche actions condempned and mo
che profitable/aswell to the kyng as to euery of his subget=
tes. that theym wyll sue & maynteene yf the same actions so
sued & comenced myght be truly pursued wythoute coupn or
collusion. But now is so comenly vsed within this reame

that if ony ſuche offẽder offendyng in cauſer wher ony of
the ſayd actyons lie/than the ſayd myſdoers or offendeꝛs in
eſcheweyng to leſe the ſaid penaltees wyll cauſe an action po=
puleꝛ to be cõmenced apenſt cheym/by coꝟy of the pleyntif
ꝟpon that caſe. wherin they haue ſoo offenced/Or elles yf o
ny ſuche action populer be cõmenced apenſt ony ſuche ſayd
offender by gode ſeyth. than the ſame offender wyll delay the
ſayd action other by none apperaũce. oꝛ by traverſe. and han
gyng the ſame action the ſame offender wyll cauſe like ac
tion populeꝛ to be bꝛought apenſt hym bi coupn foꝛ the ſame
cauſe ꝗ offence. that the fieſt action was ſued/And than bi
coupn of the pleyntyf. in that ij. action he wyll be condempned
other bi confeſſion ſeyned/triel oꝛ releſe/ Whiche condempnaci
on oꝛ releſe ſo had by colluſion ꝗ coupn pleted by the ſaid of
fender ſhall barre the pleyntyf. in the action ſued in gode ſe=
yth/ and by thiſe ſubtyl meanes of colluſion ꝗ coupn the ſa=
id good actes ꝗ ſtatutes full ſeldom ben executed apenſt ſu=
che offenders/ Whiche cauſeth theim to be bolder to offende the
kyng/ aſwel in bꝛekyng of the ſayd ſtatutes lawes ꝗ peas.
as in robbyng murdryng exactiõs takyng quarelles mai=
tenyng. and the kyngis pour ſubgettes by extorcion ꝗ ma=
ny other vnlawful meanes oppꝛeſſing/ Therfore the kyng
our ſayd ſouerepne lord in refourmyng of the prempſſes bi
thadupce ꝗ aſſent of the loꝛdys ſpirituell ꝗ temporell/ and
at the requeſt of the ſaid comens in this ſaid preſente par=
liament aſſembled ꝗ by auctorite of the ſame hath ordeyned
ſtabliſhed ꝗ enacted/ that if ony perſone oꝛ perſones hereafteꝛ
ſue wyth good ſeyth ony action populer/ and the deffendaũt
oꝛ defendaũtes in the ſame action plete ony maner of recoue
re of action populer in barre of the ſayd action/ oꝛ elles that
the ſame defendaũt oꝛ defendaũtes plete that he oꝛ they before

that tyme barred ony suche pleyntif oz playntifes in ony su
che action populer/that thêne the playntyf or pleyntifes in ý
action taken wyth good feyth may abarre that the said reco
uere in the sayd action populer was had by coupn/or elles
to abarre that the sayd playntif or playntifes was oz were
barred in the sayd action populer by coupn/ that than yf af=
terwarde the sayd collusion or coupn soo abarred be lawful=
ly fouden/the pleyntif or pleyntifes in that action sued with
good feyth shall haue recouere accordyng to the nature/ of
the action and execucion vpon the same/In likewyse & effec
te as though noo suche afore had be had/ And ouer that
it is enacted & ordeined by thanctorite aforsaid / that in eue
ry suche action populer. Wherin the defendaunt or defendaun
tes shal be lawfuly condempned or atteyned of coupn or col
lusion as is aforsayd / that euery of the same defendauntes
haue enprisonement of ij. yere by pocesse of capias and ot
lagat to be sued wythin the yere after suche iugementes had
Or at ony tyme after tyll the sayd defendaunt oz defendau=
tes be had & enprisoned as is aforsayd/ And that aswel at
the kyngis sute/as of euery other that wylse sue in that be=
halfe. And that noo release of ony comen persone here after
to be made. to ony suche partie wheder before or after ony ac
tion populer oz endytment of the same had oz comenced oz
made hagpyng the same action be in ony wyse auaylable/ or
effectuel to let or to surcease the sayd action edytement pos
cesse or execucion . Prouyded allway that noo playntif or
playntyfes be in ony wise recepued to abarre ony coupn in o
ny action populer where the poynt of the same action oz el
les that coupn or collusion haue ben ones tried or lawfully
fouen. wyth the pleyntif or pleyntifes or ayenst theim. by try
all of xij men/ and not otherwyse/

                                      ð ß

¶ Item for kepyng of frye of fysshe of
the see in Oxforde hauen/

¶ Item where dyuers statutes & ordenaunces for sauynge
& kepyng of frie & brode of fysshe in fresshe ryuers of this rea
me before this tyme haue ben made & ordeyned. But for sauin
ge & kepyng of frie & brode of fysshe resortyng out of the see
and salt waters in to hauens & crekes wythin the sayd re
me/ony ordenaunce generall hath not be purueyed ne made
howh be it hit were full requysite and profytable to al the co
mens of this reame/and specialy to the kyngis subgettes &
inhabytantes nygh adiunyng to the Nasse & hauen of Or
forde in the countie of Suffolke/Wythin whiche nasse & hauen
there is yerely grete multytude of spawne & brode of all ma
ner fysshes of the see/ And there wolde largely encrease &
multypplie, yf they myght there conuenyent tyme. be suffred
to abyde/But now it is soo that in late dayes for a singuler couetise & lucre in takyng of a felwe grete fysshes certeyn
persones haue vsed to set & ordeyne/certeyn botes called stall
botes festened wyth anckes hauyng wyth theym suche maner vnresonable nettes & engynes/that almaner frie & brode of fysshe in the sayd hauen multeplied is taken & distroy-
ed, as well grete fysshes vnresonable as the sayd frye & brode
to nombre innumerable. Wyth the whiche frie & brode the
sayd persones wyth parte therof fede their hogges/and the re
sidue they put & lay it in grete pyttes into the grounde/Why-
che elles wolde torne to suche perilous infection of eyre that
noo persone thider resortynge sholde it abyde or suffre. to the
grete hurt of the kyngis liege peple wythin this reame/and
specially to the kyngis subgettes and inhabytantes wythin the shire of Norfolke & Suffolke/And also causeth gre
te scarsite of fysshe in that countrees. Where afore this tyme

was wounte to be greate plente. Wherfore the kyng our sa=
yd souereyne lord of his noble grace. by the aduyce & assent
of the lordis spirituell & temporell/ and at the prayer of the
sayd comens in the sayd parliamente assembled/and by auc
torite of the same/ hathe ordeyned stablisshed & enacted/that
all suche stalle botes nettes & engynes aforsayd from the fir
ste daye of Aprill, that shall be in the yere of our lord. M.
CCCC.lxxxx.be not occupied nor vsed for the destroyeng
or takynge of ony frye or broade of fysshe/ wythin the hauen
aforsayd vpon peyn of forfepture of v li. at euery tyme that
ony persone/shall happen to do contrarie to this ordenaunce.
thone halfe therof to be to the kyng/ And the other halfe to
hym/that shal happen to fynde the same forfepture/and she=
we the same by informacion in to the kynges eschequer/the
re to be determyned after the cours of the same courte/And
ouer that it is ordeyned by the auctorite aforsayd that the
Iustyces of peas of the shires of Norffolke & Suffolke.
for the tyme beyng haue auctorite & power to enquere in the
ir seuerall sessions of al the botes nettes & engynes vsed or
occupped contrary to this ordenaunce aforsayd/And the of
fenders therin before theym presented to punysshe.as by their
discrescion shall be thoughte lawfull & resonable/ This ac
te and ordenauce to endure vnto the begynnyng of the nex
te parliamente/

⸿ A bylle atte the sute of browderers
⸿ Item in the sayd parliamet it was shewed vnto the kin
ge our souerepn lorde bi the wardeyn & felishhip of browderers
in the cite of london and of euery other cytie towne & place
of this Reame/ That were thorough mynysshynge of the

Weight of Uenyce florence and Jeane golde and the Untrue
packyng therof aswel the sayd browderers as other the kyn
gis subgettes byers of browded werkes wythin this reame
susteyn ꝗ bere grete los hinderauce ꝗ dysauautage. for where
in tymes past the poude weyght of golde of ony of the sayd
coutrees of Uenyce florence ꝗ Jea ne was woute to kepe the
full weyght of xij. Unces/and thene comenly solde at xxvij.
shelinges iiij d. or thire aboute/the golde packed whiche they
now selle for a poude weight weyeth not aboue Uij. Unces ꝗ
solde for iij.li sterling the packe/ And also the bryngers in
to this reame of the sayd golde soo deceyuable ꝗ Untruly pac
ken the said golde that the threde ꝗ colour Under the first shelb
is gretter ꝗ courser thene is shelbed in sight ꝗ not accordyng
to the outwarde shelbe. to thutter enpouershyng of the sayd
browderers. and also grete charge ꝗ disauautage of the biers
of browded werke as is afor said Wherfore the kyng our fa
yd souereyne lord by the aduyce and assente of the lordys
ꝗ the comens in this present parliamet assebled/and by auc
torite of the same/ hath ordeyned establisshed ꝗ enacted that
noo persone what degre or condycion he be from the fest of es
ter that shall be in the pere of our lord M.CCCC.lxxxv.
bryng ꝗ put to sale wythin this sayd reame ony golde of Ue
nyce florence or Jeane/as or for a poude weyght/but yf the
same golde soo put or offred to sale for a poude weight/con
teyn in the weight fully xij Unces And also that the same
golde so packed be in gretnes of threde ꝗ colour wrought ac
cordyng to the outwarde shelbe. therof Upon peyn of forfeitu
re of the said gold solde or put to sale for a poude weight not
beeing fully xij Unses or not wrought in gretnes of thrude
in colour accordyng to the outwarde shelbe. or elbs the Ualue
therof/thone half of the said forfeiture to be to the kyng our

souereyn lord/and thother halfe to hym or them of his subgettes that shal sease & proue the same forfeitures by actios
of det at the comen lawe/or by byll or plepnt. after the custume of cite or towne where shall fortune ony suche forfeptu
res to fall & be/In whiche actions the defendaut shall not be
admptted to do his lawe/nor ony essopn ne protection shal
be for suche defendaut alowed. Prouyded that this act afore
the sayd fest of Ester within the cite of london be proclamed
this act & ordenauce to endure vnto the begynyng of the next
parliament.   ¶Carieng of golde & siluer ouer the see
¶Item where in a parliamet begon & holden at westmyn
ster the xvj day of Januarij in the xvij. yere of kyng edwar
de the iiij. amonge other it was ordepned by auctorite of the
same parliamet/that noo psone shold carie ne make to be ca
ried out of this reame or wales from noo part of the same o
ny maner of money of the copgne of this reame nor money
of the copgne of other reames londes or lordships nor plate
bessel masse bullion nor iuelles of golde garnesshed or vn-
garnpsshed or of siluer without the kyngis licence. But suche
persones as ben dispensed wythin the statute made in the ij.
yere of the repgne/of the kyngis blessed vnele kyng henri the
vj. and other diuers statutes made vpon xpn of felonye.
& to be demed & reputed as a felon/the same felonie to be herde
& determpned in like maner & fourme & afore suche persones
as other felonyes vsuelly were herde & determpned wythin
this reame/as in the said statute more pleinli doeth apere. the
whiche statute & ordenauce was made to endure from the fes
of Ester in the xviij. yere of the repgne of the sayd kynge Edwarde the fourth vnto the ende of seuen yeres then
next ensupng sithen the whiche vij. yeres exspired/the gold
& siluer of the coigne of this reame hath & daily is & ben ca-

riee & conueyed in to flaūdres normandie bretayne burdeaur
yrlonde. and other parties beyonde the see/ aswel by marcha
unt strangers as by deynszens/ to the grett enpouershynge
of al this reame/ and gretter is like to be wythout remedie
therfore hastly be prouyded. The kyng our souereyne lorde ꝑ
prempsses considered by thaduyse of the lordes spirituell &
temporell. and at the prayer of the comens in this presente
parliament assembled/and by auctorice of the same hath or
deyned stablisshed & enacted. that the sayd statute made in the
sayd ꝑviij. yere of kyng edwarde the iiij. be & stonde a statu:
te good & effectuel with all the prempsses in the same/and
be obserued kept & put in due execucion from the fest of the
purifycacion of our lady that shall be in the yere of our lor
de god M.CCCC.lꝓꝓiꝓ.and to endure vnto the ende of
xv. yere neꝓt sueyng/ And ouer that by the same auctorite
it is ordeyned & enacted that noo persone dwellyng or inha
bityng wythin this reame from the sayd fest of purifycaci:
on paye or deliuer wyttyngly by way of eꝓchaūge or other:
wyse to ony marchaūt or other persone stranger borne oute
of the kyngis obeysaunce for ony marchaūdise or wares or
in ony otherwyse ony maner peces of golde coygned in this
reame or in ony other reame or ony plate vessell masse bul
lion, ne Juely of golde wrought or vnwrought vpon payn
to forfeyte & lose the double some or double value of al suche
money of golde coyned plate vessell masse bullion or Juel
of golde or siluer payed deliuered or eschaūged contrarie to
this acte/ The one halfe of the same forfeyture to be to the
kynge or souereyne lorde/and the other halfe to ony of his
subgettes that wylle sease it or sue for ony suche paymente
deliueraūce of eschaūge made or to be made cōtrarie to this
act/and ꝑ it be leful to ꝑ kingis subgettes in this cause to
                                                        sue

for the sayd forfeyture by action of dette by wryte at the co
men law by bylle or playnt after the custume of y̆ cite por
te or towne where it shall happen ony forfeyture to falle/ &
be/or by Informacyon to be made in the kyngis eschequer
And that noo protection nor essoine be alowable in ony su
che action or informacyon/

Nota de finibz

Item where it is ordeyned in the tyme of kyng Edwar
de the first by the statute de finibz that notes & fynes to be le
uyed in the kyngis court afore his iustices sholde be openly
& solempny rede. And that plees in the meane tyme sholde
cease. And this to be done by two dayes in the weke/ after
the descrecion of the Iustyces, as in the same statute more
pleynly appereth/ The kyng our sayd souereyn lorde conside/
reth that fynes ought to be of the grettest strength to avoy
de stryues & debates and to be fynall ende & conclusion and
of suche effect were take afore a statute made of none clay
me/ and now is vsed the contrary to the vnyuersall trouble
of all the kyngis subgettes Wylle therfore it be ordeyned
by the aduyse of the lordis spirituell & temporell and the co
mens in the sayd parliament assembled/ and by auctoryte
of the same/that after the ingrosing of euery fyne to be leup
ed.after the fest of Ester that shall be in the yere of our lord
M.CCCC.lxxxx.in the kyngis courte afore his Iustices
of the comen place/of ony londes tenementes or other heredy
tamentes the same fyne be openly and solempny rede & pro/
claymed in the same courte the same terme/and in iij.termes
thenne next folowyng/ the same ingrosyng/in the same cour
te/atte iiij. seuerall dayes in euery terme And in the same
tyme that it is soo rede & proclaymed all plees ceasses and
the sayd proclamacions soo had and made / the sayd fyne to

be fynall ende and conclude as well pryuees as estraugers
to the same. Excepte wymmen couert other than ben parti=
es to the sayd fyne   .And euery persone theme beyng
wythin age of xxj. yeres/in prysone or oute of this reame.
or not of hole mynde/at the tyme of the sayd fyne skuped not
parties to suche fyne.And sauyng to eueri persone or perso
nes & to their heires other thene the parties in ye said fyne su
che right clayme & interest, as thei haue to or in the sayd londes
tenementes or other heredytamentes tyme of suche fyne in=
grosed. Soo that they pursue their title claym or interesse, by
way of action or lawfull entre wythin v. yeres next after
the sayd pclamacions had & made.And also sauyng to al o
ther persones suche action right title clayme & interesse in or
to the sayd londes tenementes or other heredytamentes as
first shall growe/remayn or descende or come to theym after
the said fyne engroed & proclamacion made/bi force of ony
yefte in the taplle/or by ony other cause or mater had & made
&fore the sayd fyne skuped. Soo that they take their action
or pursue their sayd right & tytle accordyng to the law/with
in v. yeres nexte after suche action right tytle/clayme or in=
teresse to theym accrued descended remayned fallen or come/
And that the sayd persones & their heyres may haue their sa
yd action ayest the pernour of theyr pfetes of the said londes &
tenementes & other heredytamentes tyme of the sayd action
to be taken/And yf the same persones at tyme of suche acty
on right & title accrued descended remained or come vnto the
ym by couert de baron or wythin age.in prisone or oute of
this londe or not of hole mynde . That thene it is ordeyned
by the sayd auctorite that their action right and title to be re
serued and saued to theym and to their heyres vnto the tyme
they come and be at theyr full age/of xxj. yeres out of prison
Wythin

this londe vncouert & of hole mynde/Soo that they or theyr
heyres take their said actions or their lawfull entre accordynge their right & title wythin v. yeres nexte after that
they come & be at their full age oute of prison wythin this
londe vncouert & of hole mynde/ And the same actions pur
sue or other lawfull entre take/accordyng to the law/And
also it is ordeyned by thauctorite aforsayd that all suche per
sones as be couert de baron not partie to the fyne/and euery
persone beynge wythin age of xxj. yeres in prison or oute of
this londe or not of hole mynde/at tyme of the sayd fynes le
uyed & engroced/and by this sayd act afore except hauyng o
ny right or title or cause of action. to ony of the sayd londes
& other enhabitamentes that they or their heyres inheritable
to the same/take their sayd actions or lawfull entre accor
dyng to their right & title wythin v. yeres nexte after they co
me & be of ful age/of xxj. yeres out of prison vncouert with
in this londe and of hole mynde/ and the same actyons sue/
or their lawfull entre take.& pursue accordyng to the lawe
And yf they do & take not their actions & entre.as is afor
sayd that they & eueri of theym & their heires/and the heires
of euery of theym be concluded by the said fynes for euer in
like fourme/as they ben that be parties or pryues to the sayd fynes. Sauynge to euery persone & persones not partye
nor pryue/to the sayd fyne/their excepcion to auoyde the same fyne/Bi that.that thoos that were parties to the fyne/nor
ony of theim nor noo persone nor persones to their vse/ne to
the vse of ony of theym/had noo thynge in the londes & tenementes comprysed in the sayd fyne at the tyme of the sayd fyne leuyed/And it is ordeyned bi the sayd auctorite that
euery fyne that hereafter shal be leuyed in ony of the kyngis
courtes of ony maners londes tenementes & other possessions

after the maner vse and fourme. that fynes haue ben leuied
afore the makyng of this acte. be of like force effecte & auc
torite/ as fynes soo leuyed be or were afore the makyng/of
this acte. this act or ony other acte. in this said parliament
made or to be made. notwythstondyng. And that euery per
sone be at his liberte. to leuye ony fyne. hereafter/ after his
pleasure/ Wheder he wylle after the fourme contryned & ordei
ned in and by this acte/or after the maner & fourme afore ti
me vsed/

ANNOTATIONS.

Fermedowne. 1 Hen. VII. c. 1, Rot. Parl. nu. 66. For- fol. 1 recto, line 11.
medon was a writ at common law by which an heir to lands or
tenements by virtue of an entail claimed his right to recover.
"The word is derived from forma donationis, so called
because the gift doth comprehend the form of the gift : there
be three kinds of formedon, viz : the first is the descender
to be brought by the issue intail, which claim by descent
per formam doni. The second is the Reverter which lieth
for him in the Reversion, or his heires or assignes, after the
estate tail be spent. The third is the Remainder which the
law giveth to him in the remainder his heires or assignes
after the determination of the estate tail : all which you
may reade in the Register and F N B" (Fitzherbert's
Natura Brevium) *Coke on Litt* : ed : *Hargrave.*

Pernours of the profytes, Pernours, from the French fol. 1 recto, line 24.
preneurs from the verb prendre, takers of the profits.

Vourchers is when a *præcipe quod reddat* of land is fol. 1 recto, line 28.
brought against a man, and another ought to warrant the
land again to the tenant, then the tenant shall *vouch* him
to warranty. Voucher also is the calling in of some person
to answer the action that hath warranted the title to the
tenant or defendant.

Eide pyer, an error in Caxton's print for pryer. "In real fol. 1 recto, line 28.

actions the tenant may pray in aid, or call for the assistance
of another, to help him to plead, because of the feeble-
ness or imbecility of his own Estate : thus a tenant for life
may pray in aid of him that hath the inheritance in
remainder or reversion :— . . . . that is that he shall
be joined in the action, and help to defend the title."
Bl: *Com*: *B. III. p.* 300.

fol. 1 verso, line 15.
(1 Hen. VII. c. 2, Rot. Parl. nu. 69.)

fol. 2 recto, line 15.
(1 Hen. VII. c. 3, Rot. Parl. nu. 68.)

fol. 2 recto, line 22.
Merchauntes of the Staple. In early times the reve-
nues of the Crown were principally derived from impost
duties on the exportation of commodities produced in this
country. The word Staple in the sense of this enactment
signifies fixed : Ducange derives Etape, the corresponding
word in French at his date, from the old French word
Estaple "nunc Etape" Nat : Bailey derives it from
Stapel, *Dan.*; Stapul, *Sax.*; Stapel *Dutch and German.*
Ducange explains it as "Emporium forum publicum,
in civitatibus præsertim maritimis constitutum ubi merces
extrancæ publice distrahuntur." Bailey says it signifies a
public town where are store houses for commodities, also a
city or town where Merchants jointly lay up their commodities for the better vending them by wholesale. Webster
defines it as that which is fixed, or a fixed place : *the
Merchants of the Staple* were first incorporated by Edw. III.,
in whose time they had their staple of wool at Calais : the
chief staple commodity of England was for a long period
its Wool, which was in great request amongst the
Manufacturers of France and Flanders : "the Merchants of
the Staple" says Anderson in his *Historical Deduction of the
History of Commerce,* "were the first and ancientest Commercial Society in England, so named from their exporting
the Staple wares of the kingdom : it was put under sundry
regulations, and was the means of bringing in considerable

wealth, as well before as after the making of woollen cloths
here : they were privileged by many succeeding kings :
Henry III., Edw. II., Richard II., Hy. IV., and Henry V.,"
they bought the wool from the producers, and being
established in some certain place for its sale were termed
Staplers : the Netherlands being unable to grow sufficient
for their manufactures, took large quantities. The Staplers
in the 12th century collected the wool at some sea port
convenient for exportation, where they paid the king's duty.
In the year 1660 an Act was passed prohibiting the exportation of Wool, and soon afterwards the Wool Staplers
Company virtually became obsolete, having for many years
engrossed the foreign trade of England.

(1 Hen. VII. c. 4, Rot. Parl. nu. 67.) fol. 2 verso, line 1.

Ordynaries, properly the Bishop of the Diocese himself, fol. 2 verso, line 9.
but the term is used for every commissary, deputy, or
official of the Bishop or other judge ecclesiastical who has
judicial authority within the jurisdiction.

Aduoutre, adultery. fol. 2 verso, line 14.

Henry the Seventh, error in Caxton for Henry the Sixth. fol. 3 recto, l. 5 & 19.

Vj. shelinges viij. pens. The prevalence of this sum in fol. 3 recto, line 9.
legal matters, such as fees, fines, etc., arises from the fact of
its being half a mark ; the mark being one of the oldest
coins of this realm, the value of which was 13s. 4d.

To hym that fyndeth it and proueth it, etc. This was fol. 3 verso, line 1.
called suing by *action populer*, a very common procedure in
those times.

Shepes skynnes. In 1303 a complaint was made to Sir fol. 3 verso, line 25.
John le Blount, Mayor of London, and the other civic
authorities, by " many good folks," cordwainers of the City,
that certain persons of their craft were in the habit of
unlawfully mixing the leather used in their workmanship,
basil or *sheepskin*, for example, with cordwain, and calf-

leather with cow-leather, and of making shoes of these inferior kinds of leather and selling the same "to the knights and other great lords of the land" for cordwain and for kid. Sheepskins were almost exclusively used for the manufacture of gloves.

fol. 4 recto, line 3.

(1 Hen. VII. c. 6, Rot. Parl. nu. 72).

fol. 4 recto, line 3.

Fro beyonde the see, i.e., from Brittany, where Henry had resided from 1471 up to the time when he took the field against Richard III.

fol. 4 recto, line 12.

In *seintwarie or in hedyll*, in sanctuary or in hiding-places ; hidel is interpreted by Bailey as signifying a sanctuary or place of protection.

fol. 4 verso, line 7.

Dyssin, disseisina, unlawfully dispossessing a man of his lands. " Disseis is a putting a man out of seizin, of ancient time a disseisin was defined thus 'disseisin est un personel trespasse de tortious ousterdel seizen.' " *Litt.*

fol. 4 verso, line 18.

Thomas and Elizabeth Wyndesore. Thomas Windsor, of Hanwell, Middlesex, married Elizabeth, eldest daughter and co-heir of John Andrews, of Baylham, County Suffolk ; he was an ancestor of the first line of the Earls of Windsor, (not of the present, whose paternal name is Hickman.) Thomas died in 1485, and was buried in Hanwell Church, " where," says Lodge, in 1779, " is yet remaining under a cornice a raised tomb on which were the figures of a gentle-man and his lady, inlaid in brass, with an escutcheon of their arms, but are now torn off, as also the inscription."

fol. 4 verso, line 17.

Sir John Coket prest, i.e., priest. Fuller in his Church History of Britain, book VI., p. 352, ed. 1655, writes "More Sirs than Knights." "Such Priests as have the addition of Sir before their Christian names were men not graduated in the University, being in *Orders*, but not in degrees." In the life of Bishop Waynflete it is however said to have been a title given to such as had taken a degree, and the case is adduced by Dr. Chandler, of the Bishop's brother John, who was styled Sir, " perhaps as being B. A." In the buttery-books of St. John's Coll., Oxon, every Bachelor has the prefix of Sir,

(1 Hen. VII. c. 7, Rot. Parl. nu. 74.)
fol. 4 recto, line 1.

Bayle, bayliff, the bayliff errant appointed by the sheriff of the county to execute writs, summon the sessions, assizes, etc.
fol. 5 recto, line 6.

Rescusse, or Rescous in Law " is when the Lord distraineth in the land holden of him for his rent behind, if the distresse be rescued from him, &c." *Coke Litt.*, ed.: *Hargrave.* Here, however Rescusse simply means to rescue in the ordinary sense.
fol. 5 verso, line 28.

(1 Hen. VII. c. 8, Rot. Parl. nu. 70.) *Navee.* This term here merely implies the merchant navy ; there was no royal navy at that period, and, whenever ships of war were wanted, vessels of the merchant service were armed and manned. The first ship of the royal navy was the Great Harry, built by Henry VII. at a cost of £14,000, the same amount as he is said to have expended in the erection of his chapel at Westminster Abbey. (Stow, by Howes, p. 484.)
fol. 6 recto, line 11.

Guyen and Gascoygne, i.e., Bordeaux wines. See also Statute 4 Hen. VII. c. 10, which is to the same effect.
fol. 6 recto, line 27.

(1 Hen. VII. c. 9, Rot. Parl. nu. 73.) The silk-trade, which subsequently formed the main business of the Mercers, is stated in Statute 33 Hen. VI. c. 5 to have been carried on by the " silk-women and throwsters," who, petitioning for that Act, pray " that the Lombards and other strangers may be hindered from importing wrought silk into the kingdom contrary to custom, and to the ruin of the mystery and occupation of silk-making and other virtuous female occupations."
fol. 6 verso, line 9.

fol. 6 verso, line 27.

Wge or doo his lawe. This consisted in swearing upon the book that what the plaintiff stated was false. This oath had to be substantiated by six, eight, or twelve men, who attested the same, and were called compurgators. The offer to do this was named "wager of law," and to proceed in this manner was styled "doing of your law." The principal had to affirm directly the contrary of what was imputed to him, but the others merely swore that they believed that he spoke the truth. It was of no avail, however, against the King, nor was it permitted where the Plaintiff relied upon a deed, or other specialty, nor to an outlawed Defendant, or to one under 21 years of age, nor where the Plaintiff was an Infant, but it was permitted to a feme covert with her husband. In doing his law, he that waged his law, after being admonished by the judges of the nature and danger of a false oath repeated a form of oath denying the subject matter wherewith he was charged, and then eleven of his neighbours acting as compurgatory, avowed upon their oaths their belief that he spoke the Truth. The custom prevailed in the old Gothic constitution.

fol. 6 verso, line 18.

Essoyne, a plea for delay and non-appearance by reason of sickness or other just cause of absence. Five kinds of legal essoins are given in "*les Termes de la Ley*" (1641, p. 146). 1st, *essoin de ouster le mer,* by which forty days were granted. 2nd, *de terra sancta,* which lasted for a year and a day. 3rd, *de male vener,* or the common essoin, by which the suit was adjourned to a common day. 4th, *de malo lecti,* on account of sickness, for a year and a day. 5th, *service del Rey,* when the warrant had to be shown on the day, and a future date was appointed.

fol. 7 recto, line 18.

(1 Hen. VII. Rot. Parl. nu. 20.) As Bacon observes, it is evident by this statute that, "from the beginning, the King was not forgetful of his coffers, by drawing to himself the seizures and compositions of Italian goods, for not employment, being points of profit to his coffers."

fol. 8 recto, line 10.

Oost, the words of the Text at this reference are that "noo

straũger of what coũtrey so euer shoolde oost or take to
soiourne with him wythin this reame of Englond, ony
marchãute straũger not beyng of the same nacion that he
sholde be of, upon peyne, &c." This prohibition seems to
be twofold ; first against oosting the particular persons
described, secondly, against taking them to sojourn : the
meaning of the word oost is to be gathered from the act
18th, Henry VI., ch. IV., which enacts "that all merchant
aliens and strangers, from henceforth coming and abiding to
Merchandyse within any city, town, boro', or port in England,
shall be under the surveying of certeyn people, to be called
Hosts, or surveyors, to them assigned by the Mayor, Sheriffs,
or Bailiffs, of the same cities, towns, boroughs, or ports."
These Hosts were to be privy to all sales and contracts of
aliens : their fee to be 2d. in every 20s. Merchandize
bought or sold : Hosts to be sworn, and to be displaced for
misconduct : Merchants of the Hanse towns were exempted
from the requirement of this enactment.

xl. li. The founders of our legal polity, whenever they
have had occassion to fix a certain number, have shown a
strong predilection for the number forty. By the laws of
Æthelberth, one of our Saxon Kings, the term for the payment of blood-money was fixed to 40 nights. At Preston,
in the reign of Henry III., every newly-made burgess was
compelled to build himself a house within 40 days, or he
was mulcted 40 pence. Merchants from Lorrain anciently
were only allowed to remain 40 days in the City, and in
still older times no man was suffered to abide in England
above 40 days unless he were enrolled in some tithing. A
widow might remain in her husband's capital messuage for
a term of 40 days. A tenure of a knight's service consisted
in attending the King fully equipped for war yearly for 40
days. Those who took sanctuary were there in security for
40 days, and if they undertook to leave the country, 40
days more were granted them in order to effect this purpose.
Members of Parliament were protected from arrest 40 days
after prorogation and 40 days before the next meeting,

fol. 8 recto, line 14.

Persons coming from places in which epidemical sicknesses were prevalent had formerly to remain on board ship for 40 days, and hence the term *quarantine*. Nor is this preference for the number 40 confined to time only. A revenue of 40s. of land constituted a yeoman, who was anciently thereby qualified to vote for knights of the shire and serve on juries; 40s. used to be the qualification of a freeholder at an election; 40s. was anciently the limited value for causes in the County Court, the Court Baron, etc.; 40 was the original number of Knights of the Garter,

fol. 8 recto, line 20.

Carekes, carracks, or carracas, was the name given to a class of trading vessels. Ducange quotes mention of them occurring so early as 1342—Richard of Walsingham says that carrikes brought spices and wines to Southampton; and states also that in the reign of Henry V., the French, with the intention of molesting England, collected a fleet of large ships, carrikes and gallies.

fol. 8 recto, line 21.

Clakked or barbed wolle. To *clack* wool was the term for cutting off the sheep's mark, which caused it to weigh less and so to pay less customs. To *barb*, or rather *bard* or *beard* it, was to cut the head and neck from the fleece, for the same reason.

fol. 8 recto, line 21.

Lockes was what we now call Flock, from Lat. Floccus, a lock of wool; Junius has "Lock, Tomentum, Floccus, Cirrus; Flock of wool, flocus Lanæ;" Johnson has "Flock, a lock of wool;" refuse, French *loque*, a rag or tatter.

fol. 8 verso, line 21.

The second parliament was called by writs bearing date September 1st, 1488, to meet at Westminster on the 9th November following.

fol. 8 verso, line 25.

(3 Hen. VII. c. 1, Rot. Parl. 17.)

Embrasaries. An attempt to influence a jury corruptly ; severely punishable by fine and imprisonment under several ancient statutes, and lately by Act 6, Geo. 4, c. 50, s. 61. "When one laboreth the jury, if it be but to appear, or if he instruct them, or put them in fear, or the like, it is a maintenance, and he is called in law an embraceor, and an action of maintenance lyeth against him ; and if he takes money, a *decies tantum* may be brought against him. And whether the jury passe for his side or no, or whether the jury give any verdict at all, yet shall he be punished as a maintainer or embraceor, either at the suit of the king or partie."— *Coke upon Littleton.*

fol. 9 recto, line 3.

Gayoll, old French gaol.

fol. 10 recto, line 12.

Batell by the cours of the comen lawe, etc. Trial by battle, which might be chosen by the defendant in appeals of murder, robbery, felony, and in suits of right ; long since repealed.

fol. 10 verso, line 13.

(3 Hen. VII. c. 2, Rot. Parl. nu. 18.)

fol. 11 verso, line 13.

(3 Hen. VII. c. 3, Rot. Parl. nu. 24.)

fol. 11 recto, line 20.

Maynprice, maynprenable. Receiving a man into friendly custody who otherwise might have been committed to prison, giving security for his appearance on a day assigned. Those that thus remained responsible were named *mainpernours,* and the person taken into their custody were said to be *mainpernable.*

fol. 11 verso, line 28.

Wythin fraūchies as wythout. The Franchise intended here is a bailiwick or liberty exempt from the sheriff of the county, wherein the grantee only and his officers are to execute all process. Bl. Com : B. II., 37.

fol. 12 recto, line 11.

Ooñ, one.

fol. 12 verso, line 3.

(3 Hen. VII. c. 4, Rot. Parl. nu. 20.)

fol. 12 verso, line 5.

fol. 12 verso, line 20.

(3 Hen. VII, c. 6, Rot. Parl. nu. 29.)

fol. 12 verso, line 23.

Cheuysauce. An agreement or composition particularly between debtor and creditor. It was also used in the meaning of interest, or what was synonymous with that according to the ideas of the time, usury. Thus, in the Paston Letters (XLVIII. vol. iv. p. 173): "two hundred marks to be lent unto you for an half year, without any *chevisance.*"

fol. 13 recto, line 5.

Loue, error in original for *lone,* loan.

fol. 13 verso, line 18.

Reserwyng to the chyrche, etc. Thus, Statute 15 Edw. II. c. v.: "Item, it is accorded and assented that the King and his heirs shall have the cognizance of the userers dead, and the ordinaries of the Holy Church have the cognizance of the usurers on life, as to them apperteineth to make compulsion by the censures of Holy Church for the sin, to make restitution of the usuries taken against the laws of Holy Church."

fol. 13 verso, line 21.

(3 Hen. VII. c. 7, Rot. Parl. nu. 28.) In order to put into circulation the money coined at the mints, exchanges were appointed in various places from whence the newly-formed coins were issued, and in which bullion was purchased for the supply of the mint. At a very early period the exclusive privilege of purchasing precious metals was claimed by our monarchs, who appointed proper officers to whom they delegated that branch of their prerogative. The duty of these officers was not only to exchange the current coins of one metal for those made of another, but also to receive wrought silver, plate and bullion, and foreign coins, according to their fineness respectively; and as the exportation of coin of the realm was prohibited, they furnished persons going out of the kingdom with foreign coin in exchange for English, and also supplied merchant strangers coming into the kingdom with English coins in exchange for foreign. These exchanges were regulated by a table, which was hung up in the exchanger's office.

In the fiftene yere of Kynge Edwarde, etc. Errata are
numerous in this collection, but at this place the old com-
positor has been particularly careless, for not only has he
put fifteenth for twenty-fifth, but he has also left out some
lines, as appears from other sources, where the statute reads
as follows: "In the twentie fifth yere of Kynge Edwarde
the thyrde ch. 12, and a oder espall statute made in the
v^t year of Richarde the ij^de with oder dyṽse statutes made
for the same reamedy in," etc.

fol. 13 verso, line 30.

Such as the Kynge shall depute. On the accession of
Henry VII., two persons were appointed to this office for
ten years, at an annual fee of £30 6s. 8d., viz., Richard
Fox and William Stafford. Richard Fox subsequently,
as Bishop of Winchester, played a prominent part in this
and the following reign. In 1509 Peter Corsy, merchant of
Florence, was appointed to this office, "the said Peter to
conduct all foreign exchanges and rechanges at the rate of
3d. for the exchange and rechange of each ducat of gold,
over and above 1d., which used to be paid for the same."
Ruding, Annals of the Coinage, vol. iv., p. 160.

fol. 14 recto, line 7.

(3 Hen. VII. c. 8, Rot. Parl. nu. 33.)

fol. 14 verso, line 6.

Wered, Valued, from the Anglo-Saxon weorth, wurth,
wyrth; worth, price, value, in L. 1 Edouardi confessoris c. II.
legitur, Were suum, id est pretium suæ redemptionis.

fol. 14 verso, line 28.

Vesses rayes sayling clothes. Sometimes, instead of vesses,
we read vesset, and in some copies of this Act the word is
spelled vesseis: whatever colour it was (perhaps the colour
of the vetch blossom), it was formerly much in use. Rayes
cloth is probably the same as cloth of ray, striped or rayed
cloth, in mediæval Latin, *pannus radiatus.* Mention of a
"ray gown" is made in the Paston Letters (CI., vol. iv., p.
421), where it is explained as "a gown made of cloth that
was never either coloured or dijed." Cloth of say is a kind
of serge.

fol. 18 recto, line 23.

---

fol. 18 recto, line 25.

(3 Hen. VII. c. 15, Rot. Parl. 23.)

fol. 18 recto, line 30.

Chaces, parkes, and warens. The difference between these three is, that the *park* is an enclosed space in which game is kept; the *chase* is larger, and not enclosed, and differs from a forest in this, that the chase may belong to a subject. A *warren* is a place privileged by prescription or grant of the King for the preservation of hares, rabbits, partridges, and pheasants.

fol. 18 recto, line 13.

Vert, In the forest laws, was everything within the forest that grows and bears a green leaf. *Over vert* were the large trees, *under vert* the underwood. Trees that bear fruit upon which the deer feed were called *special vert,* and the destruction of these was more severely punished than that of the other verts. A ballad of the early part of the 13th century begins thus:

> "Sumer is ycumen,
> &c.,
> Bulluc sterteth,
> Buck verteth.

from A.-S., a leap. Chaucer uses sterting, in the sense of leaping nimbly.

fol. 18 verso, line 18.

In his grete troubles, Alluding to the insurrection of Lovel and the Staffords, the Lambert Simnel conspiracy and the revolt in Ireland on that occasion.

fol. 19 verso, line 2.

Dibdin considers this article on the price of long-bows to be a chapter with the title omitted, which it obviously is; the statute passed in the third Parliament of the king, regulating the price of cloth, is also without a title.

fol. 19 recto, line 13.

Conysaûce. The badge or cognisance was the master's crest, supporter of his arms, or other heraldic emblem, worn in the cap or on the chest. Thus Henry's cognisances were the dragon, the greyhound, the hawthorn-tree, the portcullis, the falcon and fetterlock, the combined red and white rose, etc.

(3 Hen VII. c. 13, Rot. Parl. nu. 31.) fol. 19 verso, line 1.

(3 Hen. VII. c. 14, Rot. Parl. nu. 26.) fol. 19 verso, line 19.

As now late, viz., in the Simnel conspiracy, which it was thought had been fostered and countenanced by the Queen Dowager, and in which John Earl of Lincoln and several other nobles had been deeply implicated. fol. 19 verso, line 28.

Sad and discrete psones. Sad, in old English, was synonymous with serious: "My father and the gentleman are in sad talk," Winter's Tale, iv. 3 ; also in Roger Ascham's Schoolmaster, p. 27 : "Rather than for anything in it which should helpe good sad studye." fol. 20 recto, line 10.

Exspiratur. (3 Hen. VII. c. 16, Rot. Parl. nu. 22.) This Act in Rot. Parl. is entitled, "An Act to enable feoffes in trust to sue for y⁰ benefytt of y⁰ Feffors although they be outlawed." fol. 20 verse, line 1.

At the end of the fourth year 148⁸⁄₉ the King called his third parliament, but the express time is not mentioned in Dugdale, for the summons to this parliament was not to be found on the roll. However, the statute-books say it began 13 Jan. 148⁸⁄₉, and was, on the 23rd of February following, prorogued to 14th October, 1489, or 5 Hen. VII., in which session were passed the Acts numbered chap. 1 to 7 of the Statutes. On the said 14th of October the parliament met, and sat until 14th December following, and was then prorogued to January 25 ensuing, 14⁸⁹⁄₉₀, in which session were passed the two Acts numbered chap. 8 and 9 of the Statutes. And on the said 25th of January the parliament met, and sat until 27th February following (5 Hen. VII.), 14⁸⁹⁄₉₀, and fol. 21 recto, line 1.

was then dissolved, in which session were passed the Acts numbered chap. 10 to 24. The whole of these Statutes is always cited as 4 Hen. 7. It was not until the year 1752 that the new computation came into use in England, by the adoption of the Gregorian method, although it had long prevailed in Italy, Spain, Portugal, and Switzerland, Germany, and Holland, Russia still maintains the Julian style : when the old style prevailed in England, the year commenced on the 24th March, hence the reason of subsequently writing any date on or after the 1st June, or before the 24th March, 170⅞, meaning the year 1709 according to the new style, the year 1708 according to the old style.

fol. 21 recto, line 11.

(4 Hen. VII. c. 1, Rot. Parl. nu. 19.)

fol. 21 verso, line 2.

(4 Hen. VII. c. 2, Rot. Parl. nu. 20). *Fvnours*, refiners of gold and silver.

fol. 21 verso, line 7.

London, Calays, Canterbery, York, and Durham. These five towns, with Dublin, appear at that period to have been the only places in the British dominions possessed of mints ; no British coins have been found struck in other towns during this reign.

fol. 22 recto, line 23.

Sterling. Birche, Hist. liv. : derives this term from the city of Stirling in Scotland, where he thinks sterling money was first struck. Vossius derives it from Easterling, Oosterling, a Dane. N. Bailey says that the Easterlings, Prussians and Pomeranians, in old times were artists in fining gold and silver, and taught it to the Britons ; Camden in his remains says that in the time of Richard 1st. money coined in the East part of Germany began to be of special request in England, for its purity, and was called Easterling money, as the inhabitants of these parts were called Easterlings : shortly some of that country, skilful in Mint matters and Allayes were sent for hither, to bring over coin to perfection, which since that time was called from them Sterling or Easterling.

Amelles, French *émails*, enamels ; thus, in Fletcher's Purple Island, x. 33 : fol. 23 verso, line 3.

"Heaven's richest diamonds set in amel white ;"
and in the "Dutchess of Suffolk," a. iv. :
"A husband like an ammell would enrich
     Your golden virtues."

(4 Hen. VII. c. 3, Rot. Parl. 21.) fol. 23 verso, line 17.

Saynt Gregories. This church stood at the south-west corner of St. Paul's Churchyard. It was one of the oldest churches of London, having probably been erected soon after the foundation of St. Paul's Cathedral. fol. 23 verso, line 20.

Slaughter of bestes. By a statute of 21 Edw. III. it was enacted that all cattle for the consumption of London should be killed either at the town of Knightsbridge or the town of Stratford, and that their intestines be there cleaned, and, together with the flesh, brought to town. From the preamble to that Act it would appear that, before that time, the blood of the animals that were killed in London was allowed to run down the streets, and that the offal was cast into the Thames. Things evidently had come to almost as bad a predicament in the reign of Henry VII. In the Rate-books of St. Martin's in the Fields, Westminster, frequent mention is made in the 17th century of "the Neat houses at Knightsbridge;" they are also mentioned by Dodsley, in his London and its Environs, and Nares says they remained within his recollection on the same spot. fol. 23 verso line 29.

Bocherie of Seynt Nycholas Flesshamels. St. Nicholas Fleshamels was a church in or near Newgate Street, pulled down at the time of the Reformation. It derived its name from the shambles or butchery near which it was situated. The amenities of the neighbourhood are further illustrated by the old and expressive name of King Edward Street, which Stow informs us was anciently called "Stinking Lane." fol. 23 verso, line 30.

The palays where the Kynges moost royal person, etc. The Bishop of London's palace, the name of which survives in that of London House Yard. It perished in the Great Fire, and on the site of it were built the houses now standing between the yard just mentioned and the present Chapter House. The Bishop's palace was often used for the reception of princes. Edward III. and his Queen were entertained there after a great tournament in Smithfield, and Edward V. lodged in it previous to his appointed coronation.

(4 Hen. VII. c. 4, Rot. Parl. nu. 17.) Henry was at this time preparing an expedition into Brittany, which had been invaded by Charles VIII. of France, and, much against his will, was forced to appear to go along with the public opinion of England, and prevent the annexation of that dukedom to France. Accordingly, in the spring of 1489, a small force proceeded to Brittany, under command of Lord Willoughby of Broke.

Emysson of Assises. Assise was a writ which lay where a man was put out of his lands, tenements, or any profit to be made in a certain place, and so disseised of his freehold, abolished by 3 and 4 W. IV., c. 27. "If a man which hath a rent secke, be once seized of any parsel of the rent, and after the Tenant will not pay the rent behind, this is his remedie." "And of such disseisins he may have an assize of novel disseisin against the tenant, and shall recover the seisin of the rent, and his arrerages, and his damages, and the costs of his writ, and of his plea," &c. *Coke upon Litt.* "Assisa properly cometh of the word assideo, to sit together, so as probably assize is an Association, or sitting together, and the writ whereby certain persons are called together, is called Assisa Novæ disseisinæ, so as assize is but cessio." (Sessio).

Nouel dissesin as of fressheforce. Novel disseisin is when the disseisor is dispossessed again by the person he had disseised. *Fressheforce* is a force committed by disseisement, abatement, intrusion of any land or tenement. For the redressing of this wrong he that had right might have his remedy without writ by an assise or bill of fressheforce, brought within forty days after the force committed or title to him accrued, in which action he could make his protestation to sue in the nature of what writ he liked.

(4 Hen. VII. c. 5, Rot. Parl. nu. 19.) fol. 25 verso, line 29.

On the enrolment of this Act after the royal assent, provisions in favour of numerous abbots were inserted. At the head of these are the Dean of Windsor and the Abbot of Westminster. See Statutes of the Realm, p. 530. fol. 26 recto, line 20.

(4 Hen. VII. c. 6, Rot. Parl. nu. 15. Inglewood or Englewood. William the Conqueror having dispossessed the Scotch of the County of Cumberland, gave it to Ranulph de Meschiens, one of his Norman followers. He reserved, however, for his own use a large tract in the middle of the county, between the eastern and western mountains, covered with forest, and full of red and fallow deer, wild boars, and all kinds of game. This was the forest of Englewood, which lay between the rivers of Shawk and Eden ; it extended from Carlisle to Penrith, and covered a surface of sixteen miles in length by ten miles in breadth. See the boundaries as taken in a perambulation, 29 Edw. I., in Nicholson and Burn's History and Antiquities of Westmoreland and Cumberland, Vol. II., p. 522. fol. 26 recto, line 21.

Thomas Lord Dacre of Gillisland was warden of the Westmarches. He died October 25th, 1525. The title became dormant by the attainder of Leonard Lord Dacre in 1569, for participation in the rebellion of the Earls of Northumberland and Westmoreland. fol. 26 verso, line 2.

Earl of Northumbr̃. Henry Percy, fourth Earl of Northumberland, who was in great favour with Henry VII. on fol. 26 verso, line 7.

account of his having remained neutral at the battle of Bosworth, keeping his numerous forces of Northern men from joining in the battle, which materially contributed to the overthrow of Richard III. Henry made him Lord Lieutenant of Northumberland ; he was murdered by the revolted North Country men 28th April, 1489. Skelton, in his quality of Poet Laureate, wrote an elegy on the earl's death.

fol. 26 verso, line 9.   Three other provisions are entered on the enrolment of this Act, after the royal assent, in favour of Walter Story, William Walton, and Richard Brown, Foresters.

fol. 26 verso, line 10.   (4 Hen. VII. c. 7., Rot. Parl. nu. 13.)

fol. 26 verso, line 25.   (4 Hen. VII. c. 8, Rot. Parl. nu. 25.)

fol. 27 recto, line 20.   *Saynte Thomas the Appostell,* December 21. Bacon much admired " the wise model of this Act, not prescribing prices, but stinting them not to exceed a rate, that the clothier might drape accordingly as he might afford."

fol. 27 recto, line 23.   (4 Hen. VII. c. 9, Rot. Parl. nu. 24.)

fol. 28 verso, line 21.   (4 Hen. VII. c. 10, Rot. Parl. nu. 39.) *Tolowse wood,* i.e. woad, a plant used as a blue dye before the introduction of indigo, but since completely abandoned, the indigo being much cheaper. The wild woad (French, *vaud*) was and is still used as a yellow dye. This statute is a repetition and enlargement of 1 Hen. VII. c. 8, the preamble being almost literally the same.

fol. 28 verso, line 16.   (4 Hen. VII. c. 11, Rot. Parl. nu. 40.)

fol. 29 verso, line 4.   (4 Hen. VII. c. 12, Rot. Parl. nu. 41.)

fol. 30 recto, line 3.   *Exchetours. Escheat.* It was when a tenant in fee simple had committed any felony for which he was hanged, or when he had abjured the realm, or been outlawed; or if a tenant died without heir, then the lord of whom he held the land was allowed to enter by way of *escheat*, or if another took possession, the lord could have a writ against him of *escheat*. From this term was derived the word *escheatour*, the title of an officer whose duty it was to observe the *escheats* in the county of which he was *escheator*, and notify them to the Exchequer. The escheator was appointed by letters patent from the Lord Treasurer, and the office was anxiously sought after, whence it may be inferred that it was profitable, his inquests were to be taken by good and lawful men of the county, impanelled by the Sheriff. *4th Inst.* 225.

(4 Hen. VII. c. 13, Rot. Parl. nu. 42.) Benefit of Clergy was originally strictly confined to those having the *habitum et tonsuram clericalem*, but in process of time, every one who could [show] a mark of great learning in those days came to be accounted a Clerk or Clericus, and was admitted to the privilegium clericale; this stat. was passed in order to draw a distinction between lay scholars and clerks in orders, accordingly it directs that no person once admitted to the benefit of clergy, shall be admitted thereto a second time unless he produces his orders, and in order to distinguish their persons, all laymen admitted to this privilege are to be burnt with a hot iron, in the brawn of the left thumb.

Thordynari. After the offender had delivered his neck-verse, he was finally delivered over to the Ordinary, to be dealt with according to the ecclesiastical canons, and to make purgation by undergoing the form of a canonical trial. This second trial took place before the bishop or his deputy, and a jury of twelve persons who gave their verdict on oath; the prisoner answered on oath, the witnesses were examined on oath, and twelve compurgators affirmed on oath that they believed him. On this, though the prisoner had been convicted at common law by the clearest evidence, or had even confessed his guilt, he was invariably acquitted: the neck verse was generally the first verse of the 51st Psalm (the Miserere) in a Latin MS. Psalter: but it was not always that particular verse, a more difficult one might be assigned. Otway has " He cant write his name nor read his neckverse."

fol. 31 recto, line 6.

(4 Hen. VII. c. 14, Rot. Parl. nu. 43.) Edward Plantagenet, son of Edward IV., had been the last Earl of March. When he succeeded to the Crown in 1483, as Edward Vth, all his previous titles were merged in the kingly dignity. The title was not derived from any city or county.

fol. 31 verso, line 18.

(4 Hen. VII. c. 15, Rot. Parl. nu. 44.)

fol. 31 verso, line 31.

From the brydge of Stanys, etc. The jurisdiction of the Lord Mayor and Corporation of London extends from Colneditch above Staines bridge in the West, to the Yenlet, or, as it is called in old deeds, Yenland versus Mare, in the East, and includes part of the rivers Lea and Medway.

fol. 32 recto, line 20.

Groŭde soo drowned. Not only the water, with the fish therein, belongs to the City, but also the soil and ground of it, as appears from the following memorandum found among the manuscripts of Burleigh, Lord Treasurer in the reign of Queen Elizabeth :—" Also for proof of the Prince's interest in rivers flowing from the sea, the Thames and conservation thereof was not only given to the City of London, but, by their special suit, the King gave therewithal the ground and soil under the same: whereupon, if any that has a house or land adjoining do make a strand, stairs, or such like, they pay forthwith a rent to the City of London, how high soever they be above the low-water mark."

fol. 33 recto, line 26.

Marlebridge, i.e., Marlborough. Henry III., in 1269, held a Parliament at Marlborough, in which were made what were called the Statutes of Malbridge. They may be said to have formed an appendix to Magna Charta.

Releef, an incident to knight's service, was a certain sum of money which the heir had to pay to the lord of whom those lands were held, which, after the decease of his ancestor, descended to him. The relief of a whole knight's fee was one hundred shillings.

fol. 33 verso, line 24.

Wast, for Waste, is where a tenant for life or for term of years or a guardian in chevalry doth, to the prejudice of the heir, or of him in the reversion, make waste or spoil of houses, woods, gardens, orchards, etc., by pulling down the house, cutting the timber, etc.

fol. 33 verso, line 29.

(4 Hen. VII. c. 19, Rot. Parl. nu. 48.) In the Statutes of the Realm this Act is entitled, "An Act agaynst pullyng down of townes."

fol. 34 recto, line 25.

Halfendele, A.-S. Half part: dele or deel, part. From A.-S. deel or dele, a part, from deelan to divide: this word survives in our day, in the verb deal, as to deal the cards, to divide them into parts amongst the players; and as a noun substantive in the ordinary phrase—a good deal, a great deal.

fol. 35 recto, line 3.

(4 Hen. VII. c. 20, Rot. Parl. nu. 49.) *Accions Populers.* An action popular was an action given upon the breach of some penal statute, the which action every man that would might sue for himself and the King, by information or otherwise, as the Statute allowed and the case required.—

fol. 35 recto, line 27.

Mayntenaūces. Many Statutes were passed against the offence of Maintenance.

fol. 35 recto, line 24.

Couyn, covin. A conspiracy between two or more, to the prejudice of another. Covina cometh of the French word convisie, and is a secret assent determined in the hearts of two or more, to the defrauding and prejudice of another.

fol. 35 recto, line 30.

fol. 36 recto, line 3.   *Abarre,* aver.

fol. 36 recto, line 16.   *Capias utlagat.* This was a writ in outlawry directing the sheriff to take, utlagatum, the outlaw; from A.-S. ut lage, out of law.

fol. 36 verso, line 2.   (4 Hen. VII. c. 21, Rot. Parl. nu. 50.) Orford was formerly a place of considerable traffic and importance, so as to have been able, in 1359, to send vessels and troops to the siege of Calais. But the sea retiring, and throwing up a dangerous bar at the mouth of the river, choked up the harbour, so that the trade and fishery fell to decay, and with them the town became deserted.

fol. 37 recto, line 1.   (4 Hen. VII. c. 22, Rot. Parl. nu. 51.) *Brouderers,* embroiderers.

fol. 37 recto, line 1.   *Jeane,* Genoa.

fol. 37 verso, line 2.   *Vntrue packyng.* The complaint was, that the trundles or quills of gold thread imported from Italy were deficient in weight, and made up of an inferior quality of gold thread, with a layer of superior thread over the surface, so as to deceive the purchaser.

fol. 38 recto, line 21.   *Kyng henri the vij.* Error in original for Henry VI. The "persones as ben dispensed" were those who paid ransoms for English prisoners beyond the sea; soldiers were also allowed to take a reasonable amount of money with them when sent on expeditions into foreign countries, and the inhabitants of the northern counties were allowed to pay English money for cattle bought in Scotland. (2 Hen. VI. c. 6.)

fol. 38 verso, line 7.   *Nota de Finibus.* Coke describes a fine as a final agreement which was used to put an end to suits, and says that it was made with the consent of the king, or his justices; but a note in Hargrave's edition of Coke upon Litt. says, "this gives a very inadequate idea of fines: in Glanville's time they were really amicable compositions of actual suits, but for several centuries past they have been so only in name, being in fact fictitious proceedings, in order to transfer or secure real property, by a mode more efficacious than ordinary conveyances : another use of them was to bar estates tail : the subject involves much abstruse learning." The object of this act was to ensure perfect publicity to the levying of fines, by causing them to be proclaimed in open court, on four several days in term time, and when so levied to bar all adverse claims to the lands, &c., unless prosecuted within the time prescribed by the Act. In 1833 the Act 3-4, Wm. IV., c. 74, was passed "for the abolition of fines and recoveries."

Yefte, gift.

Couert de baron. A married woman is styled in law a *femme covert. Baron* is Norman French for a husband, from the Spanish word *varo*, a man. *Vncouert*, which occurs a few lines lower, has of course a meaning opposed to covert.

fol. 39 verso, line 17.

fol. 39 verso, line 27.

INDEX.

Ingram Content Group UK Ltd.
Milton Keynes UK
UKHW011603060323
418105UK00009B/1123

9 781372 486715